2004

ETHICS AND VALUES IN HEALTH CARE MANAGEMENT

Ethics and management are often thought to be incompatible. The world of management is seen by many to be too pragmatic to allow any room for moral considerations.

This volume is concerned with exploring whether there is a place for ethics in the field of health care management and, if so, what this place is. *Ethics and Values in Health Care Management* presents a debate between those who think that ethics occupies a central place in health care management and those who deny that constructing an ethic for health care managers is a feasible project. The first group argue that the specific goals of health care management create the circumstances for the formulation of an ethic for managers. The second group stress the arbitrary nature of managerial roles and the consequent lack of scope for reasoning in a way that is appropriate to the construction of an ethic for health care managers. The volume also provides three case studies of management in health care in France, Greece and Poland, emphasising their ethical aspects.

Ethics and Values in Health Care Management provides a balanced and up-to-date analysis of the relationship between ethics and management in the health services.

Souzy Dracopoulou is a senior lecturer in Applied Philosophy at Middlesex University, specialising in health care ethics.

PROFESSIONAL ETHICS
Editor: Ruth Chadwick
Centre for Professional Ethics, University of Central Lancashire

Professionalism is a subject of interest to academics, the general public and would-be professional groups. Traditional ideas of professions and professional conduct have been challenged by recent social, political and technological changes. One result has been the development for almost every profession of an ethical code of conduct which attempts to formalise its values and standards. These codes of conduct raise a number of questions about the status of a 'profession' and the consequent moral implications for behaviour.

This series seeks to examine these questions both critically and constructively. Individual volumes will consider issues relevant to particular professions, including nursing, genetic counselling, journalism, business, the food industry and law. Other volumes will address issues relevant to all professional groups such as the function and value of a code of ethics and the demands of confidentiality.

Also available in this series:

ETHICAL ISSUES IN JOURNALISM AND THE MEDIA
edited by Andrew Belsey and Ruth Chadwick

GENETIC COUNSELLING
edited by Angus Clarke

ETHICAL ISSUES IN NURSING
edited by Geoffrey Hunt

THE GROUND OF PROFESSIONAL ETHICS
Daryl Koehn

ETHICAL ISSUES IN SOCIAL WORK
edited by Richard Hugman and David Smith

FOOD ETHICS
edited by Ben Mepham

CURRENT ISSUES IN BUSINESS ETHICS
edited by Peter W. F. Davies

THE ETHICS OF BANKRUPTCY
Jukka Kilpi

ETHICS AND VALUES IN HEALTH CARE MANAGEMENT

Edited by Souzy Dracopoulou

London and New York

First published 1998
by Routledge
11 New Fetter Lane, London EC4P 4EE

Simultaneously published in the USA and Canada
by Routledge
29 West 35th Street, New York, NY 10001

Typeset in Garamond by Routledge
Printed and bound in Great Britain by
Creative Print and Design (Wales), Ebbw Vale

British Library Cataloguing in Publication Data
A catalogue record for this book is available from the British Library

Library of Congress Cataloguing in Publication Data
Ethics and values in health care management / edited by
Souzy Dracopoulou.
p. cm.
Includes bibliographical references (p.)
1. Managed care plans (Medical care) – Moral and ethical aspects.
I. Dracopoulou, Souzy, 1951–   .
RA413. E88   1998
174' .2–dc21   98–16654
                                                CIP

ISBN 0–415–14644–5 (hbk)
ISBN 0–415–14645–3 (pbk)

CONTENTS

CONTENTS

ILLUSTRATIONS

FIGURE

TABLES

vii

CONTRIBUTORS

Kenneth Boyd is a senior lecturer in Medical Ethics at the Medical School, Edinburgh University, and Research Director of the Institute of Medical Ethics.

Ruth Chadwick is a professor of Moral Philosophy and head of the Centre for Professional Ethics, University of Central Lancashire.

Souzy Dracopoulou is a senior lecturer in Applied Philosophy, Middlesex University.

Heather Draper is a lecturer in Biomedical Ethics at the Medical School, Birmingham University.

Jacek Holówka is a professor of Philosophy and vice rector, University of Warsaw.

Thérèse Lebrune is a health economist and research fellow at the National Institute of Health and Medical Research (Institut National de la Santé et de la Recherche Medicale – INSERM) in France.

Lycurgos Liaropoulos is a professor of Health Economics and Health Care Management at the Nursing School, University of Athens.

Michael Loughlin is a lecturer in Philosophy, Manchester Metropolitan University.

Jean-Claude Sailly is a health economist and director of the Centre for Economic, Sociological and Management Research (Centre de Recherches Economique, Sociologiques et de Gestion – CRESGE) at the Catholic University of Lille.

Andrew Wall is an honorary member, Health Services Management Centre, School of Public Policy, Birmingham University.

Alan Williams is a professor of Economics, Centre for Health Economics, University of York.

SERIES EDITOR'S PREFACE

Professional ethics is now acknowledged as a field of study in its own right. Much of its recent development has resulted from rethinking traditional medical ethics in the light of new moral problems arising out of advances in medical science and technology. Applied philosophers, ethicists and lawyers have devoted considerable energy to exploring the dilemmas emerging from modern health care practices and their effects on the practitioner-patient relationship.

But the point can be generalised. Even in health care, ethical dilemmas are not confined to medical practitioners. And beyond health care, other groups are beginning to think critically about the kind of service they offer, and about the nature of the relationship between provider and recipient. In many areas of life social, political and technological changes have challenged traditional ideas of practice.

One visible sign of these developments has been the proliferation of codes of ethics, or of professional conduct. The drafting of such a code provides an opportunity for professionals to examine the nature and goals of their work, and offers information to others about what can be expected from them. If a code has a disciplinary function, it may even offer protection to members of the public.

But is the existence of such a code itself a criterion of a profession? What exactly is a profession? Can a group acquire professional status and, if so, how? Does the label 'professional' have implications, from a moral point of view, for acceptable behaviour and, if so, how far do such implications extend?

The subject matter of this volume, the ethical issues associated with health care management, is not usually regarded as the ethics of a profession in the traditional sense. Yet this is an area which has increasingly important ethical implications regarding both access to services and quality assurance. In her introduction Souzy Dracopoulou explicitly addresses the question of the relevance of ethics to health care management and distinguishes between descriptive and prescriptive approaches to health care management ethics, both of which have supporters among the contributors to this volume.

The Professional Ethics book series seeks to examine ethical issues in the profession and related areas both critically and constructively. Individual volumes address issues relevant to all professional groups, such as the nature of a profession and the function and value of codes of ethics. Other volumes examine issues relevant to particular professions, including those which have hitherto received little attention, such as social work, the insurance industry and accountancy.

Ruth Chadwick

INTRODUCTION

The place of ethics in health care management

Souzy Dracopoulou

When the National Health Service (NHS) first appeared in the UK in 1948 the managerial role within the organisation was undertaken mainly by doctors and nurses. In the two decades that followed, managerial responsibilities moved gradually away from these clinicians, as professional demands made on them increased, and a space was created for health administrators, the predecessors of today's health care managers (Wall 1989). The job of these administrators initially did not extend much beyond providing 'workshop space for doctors (assisted respectfully by nurses) to pursue their honourable calling' (Maxwell 1994). Their responsibilities were mainly to see that the 'workshop' was properly equipped and maintained, and they did not interfere with what went on inside it. As time passed and financial considerations became increasingly crucial, administrators were forced to make more fundamental decisions.

With the introduction of the 1991 NHS reforms and the beginning of the internal market within the organisation, health care administration, now properly called health care management, gained enormously in importance. The NHS was divided into providers and purchasers, with providers, such as hospital Trusts, competing between themselves in order to obtain contracts from purchasers, such as general practices. Because of this split, organisational complexity reached unprecedented levels, and specialist management skills became more than ever a necessity. The effectiveness, efficiency and economies targeted in exposing the NHS to

1

market forces have now become the responsibility of health care managers.

Just before the completion of this volume the 1997 NHS White Paper was published, proposing the dismantling of the internal market, and the replacement of competition by collaboration and a system that focuses on the needs of patients. Although the reforms will certainly have an effect on what health service managers do and who they are, especially in view of the principle, 'at the heart of the proposals', that 'decisions about how best to use resources for patient care are best made by those who treat patients' (White Paper 1997), the importance of health service management as such is unlikely to decrease.

Within this climate, in which greater importance is given to health care management (and this is not confined to the UK), the question of ethics is sometimes raised, but no extensive study in the area has been undertaken. In view of the immense interest that ethics has attracted in the context of medicine, as well as in the area of the professions in general, this might appear surprising. One reason undoubtedly is that whereas medicine, or health care more generally, with its emphasis on the promotion of health, the curing of disease and the relief of suffering, clearly provides the right environment for ethical thinking, it is less clear that health care management is receptive to ethical considerations or (and this is not unrelated) that it qualifies as a profession.

The question of whether health care management is a profession may be thought to be a difficult one to answer, as the concept of a profession is no longer absolutely fixed. With various occupations, such as accounting, teaching, nursing, journalism, trying to acquire prestige by calling themselves professions, while, at the same time, the established medical, legal and religious professions are undergoing significant changes, the notion of professionalism has become slippery. This has in fact led some to suggest that there are no such things as professions at all. But that is an extreme view. Although the boundaries of 'profession' are no longer entirely fixed, certain characteristics remain central to professions, and the extent to which an occupation becomes professionalised depends on how well it manifests these characteristics (Callahan 1988). One such characteristic is the involvement of extensive training in a certain kind of systematic knowledge and intellectual skills, which is meant to be used primarily with the community interest in mind.

Judged against this characteristic, health care management

cannot easily be viewed as a profession. It does not rest on a body of systematic knowledge, acquired in the process of formal education and extensive training, and oriented towards the public good. Present-day health care managers come from a variety of backgrounds. They do not have to be accountants and they are very rarely clinicians. They are rather a species of the generalist tradition of the civil servant (Wall, Chapter 1 of this volume). With the introduction of the 1990 NHS reforms they were brought into the NHS from the commercial world in order to manage NHS resources in a business-like fashion. Like managers in business enterprises, they are judged by the results of their work, in terms of how many economies (if not profits) they have achieved for the organisation, rather than, as it would be if health care management were a profession, by their examinable knowledge in a field (Maxwell 1994).

If health care management were a profession, then there would be no question as to the relevance of ethics within its domain. Professions are inherently ethical practices, incorporating, by definition, an ethical orientation. The question is whether there is a place for ethics as the formulation of certain moral standards and principles in the world of health care management, even if this is not a professional activity. Contrasting views have been put forward in connection with this. From amongst those which make ethics central to health care management I will distinguish the following two.

Proponents of the first view (Wall 1989; Maxwell 1994; Wall, Chapter 1 of this volume) argue that in view of some of the goals of health care management, such as responsibility for what clinicians do, allocation of scarce medical resources, rendering public account, health care managers have certain obligations to patients, to their staff, to the community and to the government, and their behaviour can and should be underpinned by certain moral principles. Working from within the context of particular managerial 'goals' or 'tasks' or 'roles', these theorists proceed to outline some of the principles underlying health care management, such as an extension of the principle of beneficence, to become the utilitarian principle of producing the greatest overall benefit (the 'constrained optimum' principle: Doyal and Gough 1991; Maxwell 1994), justice interpreted in a utilitarian way, respect for the autonomy of communities as well as for democratic processes, personal integrity. Health care managers of course rarely act out of all these principles, according to this view. But this should not support the cynics

3

who find ethics and management incompatible, but should be rather interpreted to mean that managers in health care more often than not fail to meet appropriate moral standards.

A similar position (Williams, Chapter 2 of this volume) is that it is a consequence of one of health service managers' goals, namely the allocation of scarce medical resources, that health service managers should be guided by the principle of doing as much good as possible within a resource-restrained system. 'Doing good' in this context is taken to mean improving people's life expectancy and improving their quality of life, both of which are encapsulated in the theoretical device of the 'Quality Adjusted Life Year' or QALY.

The second view is in agreement with the first, in that ethics occupies a central place in health care management and that the specific goals of health care managers determine what their ethic is. However, in contrast to the first view, which assumes a certain understanding of managerial goals, according to this second view, what the goals of health service management are is not as clear as it might at first appear. This makes it the case that 'health service management is at some kind of cross roads in its ethical development' (Draper 1996). There are at least two different ways in which health care managers could be seen (Bernman Brown *et al.* 1994; Draper 1996). According to the first view, they are seen as being similar to managers in business and commerce, differing from them only in that, as the NHS is not 'for profit', they are concerned with its financial viability (remaining in budget), rather than with profitability. After all, according to this first understanding of health care managers, NHS managers were brought into the NHS in order to improve efficiency and effectiveness, and to run the NHS like a business. If this is so, then managerial ethics in the context of health care should be indistinguishable from business ethics.

At this point the cynic might object to the idea of there being such a thing as business ethics at all. After all, the cynic might say, business is a cut-throat world where the hard logic of the market leaves no space for other-regardedness. However, it is a widely held view that ethics is central to business. One argument in favour of this is that business enterprises need to take account of all their stakeholders – that it serves long-term business interest to do so – and not just their shareholders. They thus need to take into account the interests of employees, customers, suppliers, the wider community, and not just of those who provide the finances, although in a sense the interests of those are primary. 'Employers who feel

4

unfairly treated are not going to give of their best . . . you won't get the repeat business . . . from customers who think they are unaccounted in important ways' (Vallance 1996). In view of this, according to the argument, the demands of business make moral considerations – the consideration of 'a broad range of interests' (*ibid.*) – necessary or at least 'harmonize' (Ranken 1987) with moral considerations.

If health service managers are seen as similar to business managers, then (given the understanding of business ethics above) ethical practice requires that they are concerned with patients' interests, as the interests of a stakeholder group within the NHS. But this concern is only a means to their 'business' or, more accurately, 'business-like' ends and the obligation they have to their financial stakeholders (the tax-payers) to manage the NHS well (Vallance 1996) by reducing waste and achieving efficiency (Draper 1996). Their concerns and values are thus different from those of clinical health professionals, who, by a tradition that goes back to ancient times, are dedicated to patient care.

To come now to the second understanding of health care managers and their goals, this may be described as prescriptive rather than descriptive, being concerned primarily with what the goals of health care management should be rather than with what they are. It is based on the claim (Draper 1996; Draper, Chapter 3 of this volume) that a national health service is dedicated to providing health care. Benefiting patients and maximising health are by definition its ultimate goals, unlike a private business which is primarily concerned with the pursuit of profit. Thus patient care is important for a private health care company, such as BUPA, but this is only a vital means to the company's commercial ends and not an end in itself. A private health care company, unlike a national health service, can decide to close down some of its services and use its facilities for a different purpose (e.g. turn a hospital into a hotel), if this is commercially prudent. But if a national health service is dedicated to providing health care, then (according to this view) the primary goal of health service managers should be patient care and the benefit of patients – which is what doctors and other clinicians are dedicated to. Health care managers would of course 'have a responsibility for the most prudent use of NHS resources, but rather than financial incentives, they would be influenced by the same incentives as practitioners – the satisfaction of patient care' (Draper, Chapter 3 of this volume).

It is further suggested by Draper in her chapter that the realisation of this understanding of health care management (as opposed to the business-like orientation) could be aided if managers for the NHS were trained within the NHS, rather than being brought in from business and commerce with little knowledge of health care. Moreover, if health service management took that direction, and an emphasis was placed, in what managers do, on patient care as a vocation, then it could be seen as another profession allied to medicine, with its own professional code of ethics, which is similar to, or compliments, those of other health care professionals. In addition, if health service management took that direction, the gap that has been created between managers and clinical professionals, especially since the 1991 NHS reforms, would narrow, and the tension that currently exists between the two would be reduced or would disappear.

The position put forward by Chadwick in Chapter 4 of this volume is similar to Draper's view in that it is prescriptive with respect to the goals of health service management. Chadwick looks at the individualist, communitarian and virtue ethics conceptions of the objectives of the health service and the corresponding goals of health service managers, focusing primarily on the resource allocation issue. For each of these conceptions she outlines certain moral principles, thus agreeing with the view that specific managerial goals give rise to and determine managerial ethics. But her main preoccupation is with the interpretation that each of these theoretical perspectives provides for notions that are involved in what is actually being demanded of management, such as the notions of public consultation on priority setting and provision of information to patients. It is because (as she implies) communitarianism and virtue ethics can accommodate such notions in a way that the individualist approach cannot that she seems to favour them more than individualism. In this she seems to disagree with the recently published NHS White Paper which emphasises the importance of the individualist-centred approach. In view of this aspect of the White Paper, she suggests, the government should consider how, for instance, public consultation is to be understood.

In contrast to the views above, according to which, given the goals of health care management (whatever those may be), what is and what is not ethical for managers to do can be determined, and an ethic for managers can be formulated, it has been argued (Loughlin, Chapter 5 of this volume) that the project of constructing an ethic for health service managers is in an important sense misguided. Briefly the argument is this: the goals or ends or roles of managers are shaped within the context of a social environment which is, by and large, irrational or at least non-rational. Although through our own interactions we create the social world that surrounds us, we do not control it, as our creation of it is not deliberate, not the result of forethought and rational planning. In view of the arbitrary processes that shape managerial roles (indeed the roles of any professional group or any group of people identified by their roles), there is very little scope for reasoning in a way that the construction of an ethic for health service managers requires. To say that managers ought to act in such and such ways implies the existence of reasons in favour of this statement, which (reasons) relate to managerial roles. There would of course be such reasons if the rational significance of these roles was clear – if they were created for a clearly understood moral purpose, having a place within some rational design. But this is hardly the case. Instead, they are shaped by a variety of social, historical and economic factors, which are most probably conflicting and certainly not part of a rational plan. It follows from this (according to the argument) that the project of constructing an ethic for managers, indeed any 'professional ethic' or any ethic for a group of people who are identified in terms of the social roles they perform, is an impossible one.

According to this view, the project is further undermined by the fact that (as implied in the argument above), if at all feasible, it must be philosophical; it must involve a search for some rational grounding for the moral principles that it undertakes to formulate. But if it is a philosophical project, it fails at the outset, as it is 'a key virtue' of philosophy that in its search for rational assurance it questions our most fundamental assumptions and presuppositions, and 'enables individuals to go beyond their roles'. If this is what philosophy does, no philosophical project can undertake to formulate an ethic within the context of certain social roles which are taken as given, and are hence not open to philosophical scrutiny.

Echoing in some way the view above that, given the arbitrary nature of managerial roles, there is little scope for reasoning in a way that the formulation of an ethic for managers requires, the position has been put forward (Boyd, Chapter 6 of this volume) that in the 'post-modern' world in which we now live ' "rational" solutions to "social problems" devised by experts and implemented by officials are likely to be more elusive than was often assumed in the modern era of recent centuries'. Making use of literature, Boyd attempts to show the limitations of the rational, modern understanding of the elderly and of dementia, and of the rational, modern response to the problem of health care resource allocation amongst the elderly.

I have so far outlined some of the views that fall on either side of what could be described as a debate about the place of ethics in health care management. How can this debate be evaluated?

Looking at Loughlin's views (Chapter 5, below) there is no reason why, even if it is the case that managerial roles are shaped within an irrational or non-rational social environment, there cannot be moral reasons for managers to behave in certain ways and not in others within the context of these roles. Take as an example the managerial role of distributing scarce medical resources. Even granted that this role has been shaped in an environment where scarcity is the product of various, possibly conflicting, social, political and cultural factors, rather than being the result of a rational principle, it can still be the case that there are reasons for managers to distribute resources ethically, i.e. to use them efficiently, not waste them, etc.

Loughlin's position appears to be that an all-embracing rationality is required if we are to be able to formulate an ethic to guide the behaviour of health service managers. A set of universal principles must be defended, which defines standards of correctness and incorrectness, and by reference to which, through deductive reasoning, that is through deductive application of these principles to concrete issues of practice, this ethic is constructed. The question is whether this is indeed a requirement for the formulation of a managerial ethic or, for that matter, of any ethic concerning the practices of a group of people in certain institutional roles. The so-called emotivist moral philosophers of this century would respond that, as moral judgements are not real judgements but are rather expressions of feelings, and as what appears to be moral arguments are in effect mere attempts at emotive persuasion (Stevenson 1944), this is a false requirement. The construction of an ethic, they would suggest, is not a rational project but rather involves the exertion of influence and persuasion and purports to be a 'social instrument' for the control and modification of certain attitudes. The emotivist outlook would moreover agree with or provide grounds for what is sometimes thought to happen when philosophers are invited to advise on issues of policy, such as how scarce medical resources should be rationed, where, as Brock (1993), quoted by Loughlin (1995; also Chapter 5 of this volume), says, the goal of philosophers becomes not to convince others of the truth of their views by rational means but rather to 'persuade or even to manipulate others in order to reach a desired outcome'.

Loughlin, in a different place (1994), argues against this 'irrationalist' position and its implication that rational argument is indistinguishable from mere propaganda. He criticises Hume's view on the relationship between reason and feeling, which, he says, 'provides one of the clearest statements of the irrationalist position' by rightly pointing out that, although morality would not indeed be possible unless we had certain feelings (what Hume claims), it does not follow from this that reason does not have a fundamental role to play in morals. Reason is of fundamental importance in morals, as the feelings from which morality is said to derive do not simply assail us but are open to rational assessment. Interestingly, in this same article Loughlin reaches a conclusion about the applicability of philosophy and rationality to social issues and practical problems opposite to the one he arrives at in his chapter in this volume. Whereas in his chapter below he stresses the irrational or non-rational nature of social reality and understands the project of formulating certain principles for the evaluation of the behaviour of people in a particular social setting as an impossible one, here he expresses the conviction that 'rationality is practical', that there is 'no opposition between the practical and the logical' and that philosophy should break its 'silence on important social issues', take an interest in the concerns of practical life, and 'raise the tone of popular debate'.

Emotivism or 'irrationalism' more generally provides us with one kind of negative response to the question, raised above, of whether an all-embracing rationality and deductive moral reasoning are requirements for the formulation of an ethic to guide the behaviour of a group of people in certain institutional roles. But we do not need to appeal to such extreme views in order to shed some doubt on these requirements. Emotivism, like the position of the logical positivists from which it derives, has long been discredited. If the essence of morality lies in how effective moral discourse is in its exertion of influence and persuasion, then morality is indistinguishable from mere advertising and propaganda. What we rather need is to recognise that an all-embracing rationality and deductive moral reasoning presuppose a notion of morality that is abstract, ahistorical and static. Yet morality cannot be this. On the contrary, it is an institution of life that is constantly evolving, as part of continually changing social circumstances and cultural and historical traditions. A context-free morality in which reasoning and justification are a matter of deducing certain moral judgements and certain ethical codes from pre-existing universal principles is inconsistent with the realistic conception of morality as a complex institution which is inseparable from a matrix of beliefs and attitudes of particular cultures at particular times in history. An ahistorical notion of morality and moral justification is moreover inconsistent with how moral judgements are defended and moral problems are resolved in real life. As Earl Winkler, who argues for a situational, contextual approach to moral reasoning, says, in real life the process 'is essentially continuous with the case-driven, inductive process of seeking a solution to a problem, carried out within a framework of central cultural values and guiding norms, professional functions, obligations and virtues, legal precepts, and so forth' and the methods of 'interpretation' and 'comparative case analysis' occupy a central place (Winkler 1993).

In view of the foregoing remarks, Loughlin's position that an all-embracing rationality is necessary in order for the project of constructing an ethic for health care managers to be possible cannot easily be defended. Managerial roles may very well be shaped by arbitrary processes but they provide a sufficiently well-defined context within which some moral reasoning and justification can take place. There is no doubt that contextual moral reasoning is in some sense weaker than the purely deductive kind of moral reasoning which rests on an appeal to independent, universally valid principles. However, in another sense it is stronger, as it allows for the richness and complexities of situations to be captured and thus avoids oversimplification.

This conclusion offers support to views on the other side of the debate that we have been considering, according to which, given certain managerial goals or roles, an ethic for health care managers can be constructed. However the support that it offers these theories is only with regard to their general approach and does not in any way apply to their individual and specific details. A detailed evaluation of these views is a task that I shall not now undertake.

THIS VOLUME

In my discussion of the place of ethics in health care management above I introduced Chapters 1 to 6 of this volume. Some of these chapters, notably Chapters 2, 3, 4 and 6 are revised versions (some more extensively revised than others) of contributions to a conference on health care rationing that took place at Middlesex University in September 1994. The last three chapters in this volume, Chapters 7, 8 and 9, form a category of their own in that they are accounts of the management of health care in other parts of Europe, specifically Poland, Greece and France. Jacek Holówka in Chapter 7 juxtaposes certain dissimilar systems of health care provision in order to show that they do not integrate and to support his view that the two major systems in Poland today, nationalised and private medicine, cannot happily co-exist. He argues instead for the introduction in Poland of a 'third party' system which, he thinks, exemplifies all of the characteristics ('values') that he finds essential to satisfactory health care provision, notably social satisfaction, moral commitment, economic feasibility and scientific soundness. In Chapter 8 Lycurgos Liaropoulos emphasises the ethical importance of considerations of equity and efficiency in the context of health care provision, and examines the health reforms that were introduced in Greece in the early 1980s from the point of view of equity and efficiency. Jean-Claude Sailly and Thérèse Lebrune in Chapter 9 discuss various attempts to control health expenditure in France, including schemes introduced with the 1996 health reforms. They argue that, contrary to widespread opposition on moral grounds from the medical profession as well as from the general public, such control is not unethical. Their main point, similar to the point that Liaropoulos and Williams make, is that in the context of scarcity, the pursuit of efficiency, rather than being unethical, constitutes a moral obligation.

BIBLIOGRAPHY

Berman Brown, R., Bell, L. and Scaggs, S. (1994) 'Who is the NHS for?', *Journal of Management in Medicine* 8, 4: 62–70.

Brock, D. W. (1993) *Life and Death: Philosophical Essays in Biomedical Ethics*, Cambridge: CUP.

Callahan, J. (ed.) (1988) *Ethical Issues in Professional Life*, New York: OUP.

Doyal, L. and Gough, I. (1991) *A Theory of Human Need*, Basingstoke and London: Macmillan Education.

Draper, H. (1996) 'Can Britain's NHS managers be business-like and should they adopt the values of business?', *Business Ethics: A European Review* 5, 4: 207–11.

Loughlin, M. (1994) 'The silence of philosophy', *Health Care Analysis* 2, 4: 310–16.

—— (1995) 'Bioethics and the mythology of liberalism', *Health Care Analysis* 3, 4: 315–23.

Maxwell, R. J. (1994) 'Health care management: are ethics relevant?' in R. Gillon (ed.), *Principles of Health Care Ethics*, London: John Wiley and Sons.

Ranken, N. L. (1987) 'Morality in business: disharmony and its consequences', *Journal of Applied Philosophy* 4, 1: 41–8.

Stevenson, C. L. (1944) *Ethics and Language*, London: Yale University Press.

Vallance, E. (1996) 'Ethics in business and health', *Business Ethics: A European Review* 5, 4: 202–6.

Wall, A. (1989) *Ethics and the Health Services Manager*, London: King Edward's Hospital Fund for London.

White Paper (1997) *The New NHS. Modern, Dependable*, London: HMSO.

Winkler, E. R. (1993) 'From Kantianism to contextualism: the rise and fall of the paradigm theory in bioethics' in E. R. Winkler and J. R. Coombs (eds), *Applied Ethics*, Oxford: Blackwell.

1

ETHICS AND MANAGEMENT – OIL AND WATER?

Andrew Wall

Books on medical ethics stream from the publishers but, to date, only one has appeared from a UK author which concentrates on health services managers and ethics (Wall 1989). Given the increasing role of managers in making rationing decisions, and in managing the accountability of their organisations as well as their responsibilities in controlling staff of all kinds, it is curious that there has not been more discussion on managers and their ethics.

So why is it that managers and ethics appear not to mix, to be like oil and water? Is management seen to be so intrinsically pragmatic as to be outside the scope of ethical debate? Some philosophers certainly seem to take the view that managers are somehow incapable of considering matters ethically (Loughlin 1994). Many managers are unable, Loughlin argues, to understand the basic intellectual concepts that have underpinned ethical debate for thousands of years. In reply, it is true that few managers will have studied philosophy except in the crudest manner. But that does not mean that they are not concerned with issues of right or wrong, or that they do not need to have a way of considering conflicting principles.

In today's National Health Service (NHS), managers have been at the heart of crucial decisions which require ethical principles to be rehearsed. Notable has been the case of Jaymee Bowen, a ten-year-old child with a rare form of cancer requiring expensive treatment of uncertain efficacy. The issue, in 1995, was whether or not the health authority should fund the treatment. Using the argument that the proposed treatment had a poor record of success, the chief executive of the health authority told the public, through the media, that the health authority would not be funding further treatment. It appeared that he himself was instrumental in handling the process of debate and crucial in coming to that conclusion. This case demonstrated how central managers are to ethical decisions. This may be surprising to many. They might have expected that a doctor would have been the spokesperson for the decision or that the chairman of the health authority would have fronted public debate (Wall 1995).

Whether or not this case was handled in the most appropriate way, there remains a debate as to the legitimacy of managers to be centrally engaged in matters of medical priority setting. Are they adequately equipped to explore such issues given the popular view that managers are primarily interested in the financial consequences of decisions rather than in any other aspects?

This chapter attempts to discuss managers' approaches to ethics and to explore in more detail whether or not they are capable of carrying the weight which seems, willy-nilly, to have been loaded upon their shoulders, in matters not only of safeguarding probity through proper administrative practice, but also in priority setting.

THE MANAGERS' WORLD

Health service managers are practical people concerned with getting things done. Resolving problems and making decisions about the use of resources is what they are there for. If clinicians could resolve their own problems, managers would not be needed. Increasingly clinicians have not been able to handle organisational complexity, where conflicting views have to be reconciled. Despite this, doctors, nurses and other clinicians have remained suspicious of managers, attributing to them a set of values which are finance-based and overly compliant to the government of the day. Some clinicians go further and suggest that managers' concern for patients is, at best, cursory. Managers, they say, seldom have to face the demanding patient and relative, and are therefore insensitive to the emotional and professional demands that these everyday interactions impose upon clinicians. But many managers are offended by this assumption that they are indifferent to patients' needs. As will be shown later, in some areas of care, managers have led advances which have substantially improved the lives of patients.

Undoubtedly clinicians are pressurised by the expectations of their patients. Managers experience different, but equally demanding, pressures. The environment for them is tough and their role sometimes paradoxical. Not only do managers lack sympathy from the general public, they are often derided by their very masters, the government. Both major political parties, faced with criticism of the NHS, too often start by criticising the growth of the bureaucracy – the Conservatives' 'men in grey suits' (sic – increasingly they are as likely to be women). Managers feel that this is particularly unjust given the implications of the National Health Service and Community Care Act 1990 which, by separating purchasers of health care from providers, has necessitated a large increase in managerial staff to make the system operable.

The 1990 Act exemplified the market ethos which was central to the Conservative Party's thinking. This ideological change was not necessarily supported by managers at the time, but, as servants of the state, they espoused the ideology sufficiently in order to implement the changes. This was a manifestation of their public duty and it may be presumed that the managers would do the same with any political party whatever their policies. Nevertheless, this support for the Conservatives' policies did not go down well with either clinical or support staff who largely opposed the changes in the years following the 1990 Act. Most staff felt that managers were not on their side. This had an adverse effect on staff morale.

Equally damaging to that sense of morale have been the changes in employment practice. In order to control finances, it is necessary to be able to adjust commitments speedily. The easiest way of doing this is to manipulate staffing levels. Therefore, if there is financial crisis, staff have to be reduced, and quickly. This has led managers to abandon some employment practices which are aimed at safeguarding the interests of the staff.

Ethically such actions have often been dubious and the effect is likely to be long term. If staff are treated as a commodity, they act accordingly and offer themselves in the market-place for the highest price they can command. Loyalty to the organisation has no place in such a transaction. Despite their current experience, many managers feel increasingly concerned that principles of good employment practice, which they will have learnt over many years, are still important.

So given the challenging environment managers now find themselves in, is there a place for ethics in the manager's world?

VALUES

How do the values which managers hold affect their work? Are these values shared by all managers? Can these values be codified into a recognisable ethic? One way of exploring these questions is to use Donabedian's (1980) well-known typology: input, process and outcome. What do we know about the intrinsic values that health service managers are likely to hold? How do they demonstrate them in their work and is the outcome the only way of judging whether they are appropriate or not?

Input

Where do people acquire their values? Presumably it is a mix of inculcated values from upbringing and more consciously acquired values matured by experience. For some, values may be largely defined by their religious belief, but for many others, values will be a melange prepared over their lives, not always consistent, and in the course of the working day probably not often articulated.

Managers in a classroom discussion away from the pressure of everyday decision-making, find it difficult to articulate their values until faced with dilemmas which will illustrate them. This supports the view that managers are essentially pragmatists and can only make sense of ethical issues within a specific set of circumstances. If this is so, guiding principles which hold good in all circumstances will have little meaning for them. Yet philosophical discussion in the field of biomedical ethics often relies on what Beauchamp and Childress (1994) have described as the 'four principles approach', an approach invoking the principles of autonomy, beneficence, non-maleficence and justice. Does this mean that there is a fundamental mismatch between the views of these pragmatic managers approaching every dilemma according to context and circumstance, and others, philosophers and clinicians, who prefer to be guided by a set of abstract principles which aim to ensure a degree of consistency of approach?

Even if this is the case (and it is dangerous to be dogmatic about such matters), is it problematic? The four principles provide guidance; they are not in themselves capable of indicating absolutely what should be done. So for instance, it is reasonable to hold the view that all dealings with patients should honour the principles of autonomy, beneficence and non-maleficence. Interpreted in context,

16

this means that a patient has the right both to receive respect for their individuality and to expect that their interests will be furthered and will not be abused. But interpretation of these principles is by no means easy. For instance, suppose a case conference is set up to discuss the disclosure by a volunteer play assistant that a child of six has displayed inappropriate behaviour in class which suggests sexual abuse. Should the play assistant, as a non-professional and a volunteer who is not regulated by any code, be invited to the case conference, a professional forum? She might be unreliable and talk about what was discussed to neighbours and friends. The child's right to confidentiality would then be betrayed. But despite this risk, the child's interests might be best served by inviting the play assistant to give a first-hand account of what she observed. The parents also have rights in the matter. The ethical dilemma is to decide which principles predominate in meeting the child's needs. How indeed are we to rank principles? Is confidentiality more important in this case than getting to the truth, even if there is a risk of a loss of confidentiality?

This example shows that principles help as benchmarks against which to judge specific cases. But to arrive at appropriate action there has to be discussion, transaction, and the judicious assessment of evidence. For managers, the sort of fundamentalism which suggests that principles are always true whatever the circumstances is of little use. Yet it sometimes seems that clinicians are happier with rules which prescribe a consistent course of action.

There are obviously considerable dangers in having no fixed point to govern conduct. If everything is contingent on circumstance, who will ever know what is right and what is wrong? Away from the daily care of patients, managers faced with the current (1996) political ideology may find it difficult to know how to address issues which arise from market competition. What to reveal and what to keep secret is a particular dilemma. Is it right that transactions about contracts for care should be discussed only in private by the Boards or, given that it is public money which is being used, does probity require such discussions to take place in public even when such revelations would effectively wreck any meaningful competition between providers? Which principles are to be observed? It is not surprising that managers find it difficult to decide what constitutes ethical behaviour.

Externally derived principles, whether those emanating from philosophers, clinicians or politicians, cannot be easily relied upon

17

to guide a manager. Perhaps he or she is better advised by their own personal value system, however varied they may be between one manager and another. But some managers would maintain that what they believe personally is their own affair and is of a different order to how they behave at work. For others, personal conscience can spill over into the working situation, particularly in quasi-political situations where secrecy is the issue.

A manager can also be faced with resolving dilemmas of conscience among other staff. By law no nurse is required to assist in a termination of pregnancy, but a medical secretary who for similar reasons of concern did not wish to type letters about patients who had terminations, lost her case against unfair dismissal on the grounds that her personal beliefs were inappropriately expressed by her refusal to undertake this part of her work. There is a suspicion that once the law is called in to adjudicate on matters of conscience, the result is likely to be somewhat arbitrary.

Managers may themselves have to arbitrate and in such a role their own values will be crucial. Supposing a nurse refuses to assist with electro-convulsive therapy on the grounds that this particular treatment, although widely used, is not altogether understood and could be said therefore to be an assault on a patient. Should the manager support the nurse and remove him or her from that duty or should he or she tell the nurse that his or her role is to look after the patient? The nurse is not, after all, administering the treatment.

There can be no one answer. The manager, like anyone else, will largely act according to his or her own set of values. Unfortunately, many people, both clinical colleagues and the public more generally, are suspicious of managers' own values precisely because they are usually undeclared. Managers in the health service are undoubtedly shy about speaking personally, but why should this be so? Their work is centred on helping others to be more effective, on solving others' problems, on predicting and planning the future of the organisation or service; all of which activities allow little scope for putting their own values to the fore. But if this is their argument, managers may be misjudging the situation. Studies of effective leadership constantly show that the expression of values, of ideals, is one of the most commanding attributes of effective leaders.

There may be a more sustainable argument against the expression of personal values and that comes from the tradition of being a public servant, whose ethic demands the implementation of government policy. What would happen if personal beliefs were to interfere with this? We may have gone beyond the myth that public servants should have no political allegiance as that would be to deprive them of their democratic rights. But it is not considered appropriate for managers in public service to advertise their politics.

Understandable though this stance may be, it can be challenged. Undue compliance with government can be seen as lacking in integrity. Many NHS staff are critical that managers do not join them in demanding more resources. Such staff may assume that managers' reluctance is self-interested because managers do not wish to offend those in power. Managers may not get the credit for honouring the principle that the duty of managers is to administer the system within the resources available; that this is a principle which demonstrates integrity of purpose.

Managers could probably do more to act as an effective agent between the government and the views of staff and communities. Some government policies are likely to have unfortunate results, so part of the duty of public service managers is to bring these to the attention of their superiors without suffering from threats of discipline for being disobedient. It must be a matter of concern that managers' sense of their own integrity is not always strong enough to speak out against policies which are likely to fail. This may be because of the essentially adaptive nature of their role, which leads them to be pragmatic, operating, it may appear, from no fixed points of belief. Managers can correct this impression by demonstrating their concern for ethics through process – the second stage of Donabedian's typology.

Process

Central to the managers' role is their accountability *to* others. They have to answer to the public who have an expectation of a health service which will respond promptly to their needs. As has already been said, managers are also accountable to the government for the implementation of policy. But equally managers are accountable *for* procedures which ensure the proper use of public funds and ensure that the law is observed. It might be assumed that these obligations require health service managers to have a code of conduct. At the time of writing (1996) they are not so regulated although there has been an attempt by the managers' professional body, the Institute of Health Services Management, to produce guidance in the form of a *Statement of Primary Values* (1994). Well intentioned, it falls into the trap of rhetoric and it might be said to have never been more than an attempt to recover esteem in the eyes of others.

For instance, the Statement says, 'The mission of the Institute is to promote excellence in health services management in order to improve health and health care.' But what are 'excellence' and 'improvement' other than 'feelgood' words? The Statement also suffers from problems of meaning: 'Managers will respect and welcome diversity amongst patient, colleagues and the public.' Tolerant and liberal in tone but meaningless out of a particular context. Indeed too much diversity could be detrimental if the issue is about the fair distribution of resources. The Statement goes on in a similar vein, making points with which it is difficult to demonstrate compliance, except in the most general way.

The problem for managers is that a professional code of conduct is not sustainable because managers are not, in the usual meaning of the word, professional. This is not to imply that they do not do their job properly; rather that there are no significant devices for regulating their work except through the processes of performance review. Anyone can become a health services manager, whereas a clinician has to study, pass examinations and be accredited as being suitable to enter the profession. Once in, they are monitored and any transgression may be punished, possibly by removal from the professional register. In addition, these professionals are defined as having an exclusive body of knowledge. Managers do not have exclusive knowledge; indeed they are generalists par excellence. Nor can they be removed for offending a code of conduct. Despite all this, they have obligations to the community they serve, to patients, to their Boards and to the government. Demonstrating these obligations is central to their ethics.

The managers' range of work is wide. Their accountability to patients is through their support for clinical colleagues but sometimes separate from it. It has been observed that patients are more willing to receive bad news than doctors are to give it. This is understandable enough as the doctor does not wish to jeopardise the patient's morale which can be crucial if they are to live with illness and disability. Nevertheless, in the interests of respecting a patient's autonomy, the patient has a right to know and the manager may have to ensure that protocols exist which guide medical staff as to what to tell when. *In extremis*, the prognosis for a patient may be so poor as to justify termination of active treatment. This is not a decision that should be left entirely with an individual doctor. The manager is not part of that decision itself but needs to be assured that the process by which the decision to discontinue treatment was made was ethically sound. The patient has to give consent, the relatives' views have to be taken into account and, finally, two doctors must be of the same mind. So the manager's duty is not only to assure that the rights of the patient have been protected, but also that the clinicians are not put into a dubious ethical position, even when their motives derive from consideration of the patient's needs.

Similar concerns surround research. It is a truism that young doctors cannot advance their careers without having undertaken research. The pressure on them therefore is considerable. This can lead to poorly presented research projects which are of little use to patients either in the short or the long term. The proper functioning of the Ethics committee is another responsibility of the manager. Such committees are largely concerned with research matters but there is a growing sense that these committees should also be concerned with wider issues such as what services should be provided and what should not. At present there are very few examples where a health authority seeks ethical advice on its purchasing intentions from other than the predominantly professionally constituted Ethics committee. The view of the person in the street is absent and while this perspective should not be allowed to obliterate others, it is worth having. There is always a danger with 'inside' committees that certain minorities will have short shrift due to inherent professional prejudice.

It might be thought that the observance of the law should protect managers from unethical behaviour. But this is to elevate the law to a position which it is not always able to hold. The law and ethics are not synonymous. There are examples where the law has been used actively to discriminate against people although, of course, this has been as a consequence rather than an intention of legal intervention. In Bath, a group of mentally ill people were resettled in two houses which were part of a new executive housing development. The health authority concerned was taken to court on the grounds that they had broken two conditions of sale. These were that nothing should be done in the house which was detrimental to neighbours and the housing development company and, secondly, that the house should not be used for business purposes. The presence of patients with mental illness was deemed to be detrimental to neighbours and business interests; and the managing of the house by the health authority (pre Trust status) was considered in court to constitute a business rather than a domestic use.

Only on appeal was the detrimentality claim rejected, leaving an ambiguity as to the status of the house as business or home. This objection was removed by changing the status of the patients from in-patients to out-patients (which made their status as ordinary citizens unambiguous) and, as some of them were not competent, arranging for the Court of Protection to manage their personal affairs. The patients remained living in the house. Such a case study demonstrates that the law does not always lead enlightened opinion, and may not thus always exemplify the ethical principle of respecting the autonomy of the individual and safeguarding his or her interests, unless a view is taken that the patients' interests in this case were secondary to those of the neighbours and the housing developers.

This particular case was led by the chief executive of the health authority, not by clinicians. Acting as advocate of patients' interests is another role for the manager and a rewarding one. Less rewarding may be the manager's relationships with staff, particularly, as mentioned above, in a climate of financial pressure and with the emphasis on performance as the pre-eminent value. In this respect managers have so far failed to convince staff that they are governed by ethical standards which respect staff whatever the political climate. Summary dismissals, short-term contracts and an undue and, in the research findings at least, unproven reliance on performance-related pay as a motivation, all these have taken their toll in the NHS of the last few years. This, together with the loss of power of the formal staff representatives, has left managers exposed to the criticism that they treat staff badly.

These accusations are often difficult to rebuff, and demonstrate more clearly than in any other area of managerial work, how the standards of some managers have slipped below an acceptable level of ethical behaviour. Are the relationships with the public as bad? Here the signs are more equivocal. On the one hand, some members of the public think that managers, in return for high wages, are prepared to dismantle the NHS by introducing gradual privatisation. But there are also many signs of health authorities and Trusts endeavouring to work much more closely with their communities and demonstrating that health service managers are only the agents of the public's wishes.

Managers in the public health service are required to be stewards of public resources and protectors of patient interests. They have not always reached adequate ethical standards in line with the principles of respecting rights, not doing harm, positively doing good and being just. Their reputation has suffered accordingly. But it has been argued above that context and circumstance alter cases and, useful though the principles are as guidance, it is only by exploring their application in particular circumstances that ethical action can be determined. As has been said, this may seem to suggest an unacceptable degree of pragmatism but it is the position which most managers will assume.

Outcomes

Patients, staff and the public all have expectations as to how managers should behave. These may be unreasonable in view of the complexities and some of the paradoxes in health service managers' jobs. One way of aligning expectations would be to concentrate on results. If the outcomes are good, is not that the most important thing? Ethics has long explored this approach and its practical attraction, in the context of health management, is that providing the results are good, it is not necessary for the process also to be good.

The current ideology surrounding the consumer tends to endorse this approach. Consumers are not interested in the manufacturing process when buying goods, so, by analogy, why should they have to concern themselves with the day-to-day work of managers providing the outcome – the successful operation, the confirmed out-patient appointment, the balanced financial account – is to their satisfaction?

Evidence-based medicine also endorses this approach in that it requires that only those interventions that have been proven successful should be undertaken. This seems like common sense in so far as it goes. But it does not help many patients whose diagnosis is not clear or who need to be supported through a chronic or a terminal condition where there is no hope of recovery, in other words where the results are ultimately bad.

Indeed the outcomes approach is limited in every respect. Accountability requires public sector managers not only to get good results but also to demonstrate through process that they are conscious that the means are as important as the ends. This is what the public expects in a democratic society. So, even if the ends were satisfactory, it would not be ethical for managers to advantage themselves financially in the process. Being part of a public service requires a more formal acknowledgement as to proper behaviour. Managers in the health service are custodians of public money and stewards of the public good.

A recent example illustrates the unsatisfactory nature of concentrating on results rather than processes. Three patients were awaiting non-urgent heart operations in a hospital in the north of England. They were booked for admission in the eleventh month of their wait on the waiting list, just in time to be within the regional target endorsing government's wishes that all patients should be admitted within twelve months of being placed on the waiting list. The hospital in question, a tertiary centre, then had an outbreak of infection requiring the relevant ward to be closed. An appeal to the regional office for the target to be relaxed was unsuccessful and the operations were accordingly done in a private hospital at a considerable increase in cost. The decision was made by managers and one could conclude from this example that managers are ethically adrift in a sea of pragmatism conditioned only by political obedience: they opted for observing the target that the government had set at the expense of conserving public resources and maximising the potential benefit to patients overall. However this judgement could be unduly cynical. It could be said that this example illustrates a case where managers were faced with and had to resolve a difficult moral dilemma arising from two conflicting obligations: implementing the government policy and making the best use of public resources.

The conclusion so far is that managers need to be prepared for their role by being clear about the ethical implications of input, process and outcome. There remains the issue as to whether managers are as necessary to the proper running of the NHS as they themselves would maintain.

THE MANAGER'S ROLE

Managers are faced with contradictory pressures: obedience to their masters, support for clinicians, maximising public benefit, respecting the rights of patients; all these can be, at times, in opposition. Managers may have little capacity for philosophical dialectic but this does not mean that they do not desire to do the right thing.

Nevertheless they may be hesitant at declaring their own values, fearing derision for being too subjective and not therefore exemplifying the rational paradigm associated with managerialism. Their desire to endorse proper practice is given considerable scope through procedures, policies and protocols, but these are not self-fulfilling and wrongdoing is not automatically eliminated.

The general manager, i.e. someone who does not come from a clinical background, is relatively new to the NHS and his or her counterpart is not found in health systems everywhere. In the NHS, the majority of such managers do not have a clinical qualification but neither are they necessarily accountants by original training. The tradition is more the generalist tradition of the civil servant. Most senior managers tend to be the product of a national training scheme which mostly recruits from newly qualified university graduates. The person specification at recruitment emphasises an outgoing personality who has a desire to help their fellow men and women, and who will have already demonstrated this through voluntary work. Given these attributes, how is it that ten or twenty years into their careers, managers are often characterised by their clinical colleagues as being self-interested, insensitive and motivated by a set of values far removed from those shared by clinicians? Is it that the demands of the role eventually corrupt managers, or is it that others do not sufficiently understand the manager's role?

The argument in favour of the general manager is that the organisation cannot operate effectively without the oiling of the wheels that general management provides. After all – the argument goes – if you professionals could manage on your own, why didn't you? Managers scarcely seized power; they had it given to them because, apparently, the organisation increasingly could not manage on its own. This is understandable; the organisation has changed over the years. The increasing number of clinical specialities, the speed with which many patients are now put through the system, the size of the budget, the requirements of the government, all these demands need someone who is not primarily involved in patient care. Additionally, complex organisations need leadership so as to maintain a sense of direction and to endeavour to develop a culture recognisable to staff and patients alike.

This is to make great claims for managers, claims which many clinicians and other staff might endorse in theory but question in practice. Instead, these clinicians report experience of unresponsive bureaucrats unable to inhabit the world of clinical practice, and with little sympathy for the pressures which patients and their relatives put upon clinical staff. Compliance with government policy and the overriding imperative of living within financial limits seem, to these critics, to be the governing characteristic of today's health service managers. And if this is so, the notion that managers have a concern for ethics appears merely laughable.

There is therefore a dangerous gap between the managers' own perception of their obligations and what many, if not all, clinicians perceive. In their turn, patients and the public are more likely to echo the views of these clinicians than to have sympathy for the managers. This gap in perception can only be bridged by a clearer statement of managerial ethics.

MANAGERIAL ETHICS

Health service managers need to pay more attention to the ethical components of Donabedian's typology: input, process and outcome.

Input The expression of personal values is legitimate and it is important that managers should own up to what they really feel rather than conform to what they assess it is expedient to say. An exercise in ranking the priority of treatment of six patients, undertaken by the author as part of development courses for managers, has demonstrated repeatedly that socio-economic values carry more weight than, say, respect for our elders. (Interestingly clinicians and lay people who have undertaken the same exercise endorse these priorities.) So an elderly woman waits in the queue to let a working man with children have treatment before her. This may of course, be acceptable, but it is worth exploring why our society rewards the working man before the old and frail who, it could be argued, should also be rewarded for the life they too have led as parents, and as working people. Often such values are almost subliminal but as they inform decisions they need to be recognised and debated.

Even if managers and clinicians share similar socio-economic values, they are less likely to agree as to the application of some of the fundamental guiding principles. Indeed, their perspectives are different. A manager is more likely to espouse the utilitarian principle of maximising benefit to the greatest number whereas the clinician is more committed to his or her obligations to the particular patient being treated at the time.

Managers appear to have more difficulty than clinicians in declaring their own views and may endeavour to remove the personal from consideration of issues by employing a technical sleight of hand using one of the health economists' methods, such as Quality Adjusted Life Years – QALYs – to resolve dilemmas. This phenomenon has been noted before (Hunter 1993). But fundamentally such dilemmas are resolved not by numerical calculation but by discussion of values and by consensus.

Process Managers are happier when dealing with process. Their training in administration equips them to handle such matters relatively easily. But it cannot be said often enough that the existence of an agreed procedure or of a code of conduct is not a guarantee against wrongdoing, even if it does help to assess the degree of the wrongdoing. Managers and clinicians alike need to bring more to discussion than merely honouring the process.

Outcome Assessing the consequences of action in order to indicate what should be done is alluring but, as has been pointed out, it has limited value in health care. A great deal of care aims to maintain the quality of life rather than to cure a condition: this is process rather than outcome. Managers accordingly need to guard against too much emphasis on evidence-based medicine which can do little for those with permanent disability or terminal conditions. Similar problems arise with rationing. Effectiveness is not the only criterion, even if rationing is accepted as necessary and some would challenge that (Mullen 1995). It is vital that people's values are explicit before care is denied to patients.

CONCLUSION

In the health service in the UK, managers have more power than ever before and accordingly are feared or, at the very least, disparaged. This has led to a dangerous confrontation with clinicians, dangerous because it is not in the patients' interests. But managers have themselves to blame for failing to give adequate consideration to the ethical basis of their work. Instead, they appear to many clinicians and patients alike, to be opportunists motivated by self-interest and thereby unduly compliant to political influence. This chapter, while acknowledging much of the criticism of managers' ethics, has nevertheless endeavoured to demonstrate that ethics are as relevant for managers as for clinicians. It has also supported the importance of management in ensuring that the health service makes decisions which combine the best possible benefits to individual patients with a due regard for the public good.

BIBLIOGRAPHY

Beauchamp, T. L. and Childress, J. F. (1994) *Principles of Biomedical Ethics*, 2nd edition, Oxford: OUP.

Donabedian, A. (1980) *Explorations in Quality Assessment and Monitoring*, Vol. 1, Ann Arbor Michigan: Health Administration Press.

Hunter, D. (1993) *Rationing Dilemmas in Health Care*, Research Paper no. 8, Birmingham: National Association of Health Authorities.

Institute of Health Services Management (1994) *Statement of Primary Values,* London: IHSM.

Loughlin, M. (1994) 'Behind the wallpaper', *Health Care Analysis* 2, 1: 47–53.

Mullen, P. (1995) *Is Rationing Necessary?*, Discussion Paper no 35, University of Birmingham: Health Services Management Centre.

Wall, A. (1989) *Ethics and the Health Services Manager*, London: Kings Fund.

—— (1995) 'Every manager's nightmare', *Health Service Journal*, 30 November: 24–6.

2

ECONOMICS, QALYS AND MEDICAL ETHICS[1]

A health economist's perspective

Alan Williams

Economics is about scarcity. Quality Adjusted Life Years (QALYs) are about the benefits of health care. *Medical ethics* is about the way in which medical practice ought to be conducted. This chapter is therefore about how medical practice ought to be conducted, in the face of scarcity, if our objective is to maximise the benefits of health care. This is also the crux of the relationship between clinicians (who may be doctors or nurses) and managers (who may also be doctors or nurses, but who are increasingly likely to be neither). Being a 'manager' means controlling scarce resources, human or material, and even clinicians have to play that role when organising their own professional activities. So health care management is endemic, and to appraise it we need to think carefully about objectives and who should do what to ensure that resources are managed so as to pursue those objectives as successfully as possible. This means thinking about information requirements, and motivation. But it also ultimately implies thinking about the ethical justification for those objectives. This chapter is thus both an attempt to clarify the role of QALYs as a potential source of relevant information for health care policy-making and management, and an attempt to clarify the ethical issues involved.

Common sense tells us that in the face of scarcity we should use our limited resources in such a way that they do as much good as possible. In health care, 'doing good' means improving people's life expectancy and the quality of their lives. Since people value *both* of these fundamental attributes of life, we need a measure of outcome which incorporates both, and which reflects the fact that most people are willing to sacrifice some quality of life in order to gain some additional life expectancy, and vice versa. This is precisely the role of the QALY. If some health care activity could give someone an extra year of healthy life expectancy, then that would be counted as 1 QALY. But if the best we can do is to provide someone with an additional year in a rather poor state of health, that would count as less than 1 QALY, and would be lower the worse the state of health. Thus the QALY is to be contrasted with measures such as 'survival rates', commonly used as the sole success criteria in clinical trials, which implicitly assume that only life expectancy is of any concern to people. The essence of the QALY concept is that effects on life expectancy and effects on quality of life are brought together in a single measure, and the bulk of the empirical work involved in making the concept operational is concerned with eliciting the values that people attach to different health states, and the extent to which they regard them as better or worse than being dead. For the purpose of priority setting in health care, being dead is regarded as of zero value. A QALY measure can in principle embrace any health-related quality of life characteristic that is important to people. The particular measure with which I am most familiar (the Euroqol measure) covers mobility, self-care, usual activities, pain/discomfort, and anxiety/depression. Note that 'usual activities' are whatever the individual's usual activities are, and are not restricted to work activities. So, although developed primarily by economists, the QALY is not a measure of people's economic worth, but a measure of whatever aspects of life they themselves value.

In the presence of scarcity, resources devoted to the health care of one person will be denied some other person who might have benefited from them. Clinicians are quite used to this phenomenon with respect to the allocation of their own time, and of any other resources that they control as practice managers. They are trained to discriminate between those who will benefit greatly from treatment and those who won't, and by this means 'clinical priorities' are established, which are based on some broad assessment of risks, benefits and costs. The role of costs here is crucial, because they represent sacrifices made by other potential patients who did not get treated. Thus the economists' argument that medical practice should concentrate on those treatments that are known to be cost-effective is designed to ensure that the benefits gained by the treatments that are actually provided should be greater than the benefits sacrificed by those who were denied treatment. That is what 'doing as much good as possible with our limited resources' means.

OBJECTIONS

I am constantly amazed at how controversial these common sense propositions seem to be. Priority setting is inevitably painful, and its consequences are bound to be unfortunate for someone or other. It is therefore understandable that many people cling, with childlike naivety, to the romantic illusion that if only more resources were devoted to health care, they could escape from the process altogether. But when more resources are made available, we still have to decide which are the highest priority uses to which they should be put, so this is really no escape route at all.

The more interesting and substantial objections come from those who accept the fact of scarcity, and are willing to face up to its implications, but reject the approach I have outlined. They fall into four groups:

1 Those who reject *all* collective priority setting as unethical.
2 Those who accept the need for collective priority setting but believe that it is contrary to medical ethics.
3 Those who accept the need for collective priority setting, and do not believe that it is contrary to medical ethics, but reject the role of QALYs in it on other ethical grounds.
4 Those who accept the need for collective priority setting in principle, but are unwilling to specify how it should be done in practice.

By 'collective priority setting' I mean priority setting intended to guide the use of public resources devoted to health care. I will summarise the key points at issue for each group in turn.

Is all collective priority setting unethical?

Those who reject all collective priority setting as unethical typically assert that it is immoral for one person to sit in judgement on the worth of other people's lives, which is what collective priority setting requires us to do. However, since they accept the fact of scarcity, they acknowledge that some people must be denied the benefits of health care, but they want that done in a manner which is free of any interpersonal judgements of relative worth. They believe that this can be done by recourse to a lottery. The trouble with this supposed solution is that lotteries do not fall like manna from heaven, but have to be devised and run by people, who have to determine who shall be eligible, when, and under what conditions, for each and every treatment that is on offer. So recourse to a lottery simply brings us back to the very same priority setting issues that it was supposed to avoid. They simply appear in a different context, i.e. determining who is eligible to enter the lottery, and with what probability they may win each prize.

Instead of seeking to avoid the making of interpersonal judgements of life's value, it seems more fruitful to seek as much detachment as possible when making them. An entirely different sort of lottery could have an important role to play in that process. What I have in mind is the thought experiment involved in approaching collective priority setting from behind the 'veil of ignorance'. We have to imagine ourselves outside the society of which we are members, and then choose that set of rules for collective priority setting which would be most likely to achieve the distribution of health benefits that we think best for our society. Then, and only then, will we be assigned, *by lottery*, an actual place in that society. We may find ourselves favoured by our rules, or we may be one of the unfortunate people who are disadvantaged by them, but we would have achieved a set of rules which we would have to accept as fair. The question which I would ask the reader to consider is whether, under these conditions, *you* would choose a set of rules which would maximise the health of the community as a whole, as measured in QALY terms, and if not, why not?

Is collective priority setting contrary to medical ethics?

My second group of objectors are those who accept the need for collective priority setting, but believe that it is contrary to medical ethics. In the extreme, such people believe that it is the doctor's duty to do everything possible for the patient in front of him or her, no matter what the costs. But in a resource-constrained system 'cost' means 'sacrifice' (in this case the value of benefits forgone by the person who did not get treated). Thus 'no matter what the costs' means 'no matter what the sacrifices borne by others'. This does not sound to me like a very ethical position to be in. Indeed, people who behave regardless of the costs of their actions are usually described as 'fanatical', not as 'ethical'. Moreover, if medical ethics include an injunction to deal justly with patients, then there *has to be* some weighing of the benefits to one person against the sacrifices of another. So I think that this supposed ethical conflict between the economists' argument that costs (i.e. sacrifices) must be taken into account *in every treatment decision* and the precepts of medical ethics, is non-existent, because medical ethics does *not* require everything possible to be done for one patient no matter what the consequences for any of the others.

Why might QALYs be unethical?

My third group consists of those who accept the need for collective priority setting, and do not believe that it is contrary to medical ethics, but cannot accept the QALY approach to it. There seem to be four distinct ethical issues raised here. First, whose values should count? Second, how should we move from individual values to group values? Third, should we not be concerned with the distribution of the benefits of health care across different people, as well as with the total amount of such benefits? Fourth, are there other benefits from health care which QALYs do not pick up? I will tackle each of these in turn.

Whose values should count?

Whose values should count? As a health economist it is really not for me to say. Nor, as a health economist, do I *have* to say, because the QALY concept is extremely accommodating in this respect. In principle, it can accept anybody's views about what is important in health-related quality of life, and anybody's views about the trade-off between length and quality of life. In practice, the early empirical work was based on professional judgements (mostly those of doctors). More recent work has been based on the views of patients and of the general public, and my own work has concentrated on the latter, because I am anxious to find out whether the values of the practitioners, their patients, and the general public coincide. What the QALY concept does, quite properly, is bring this question to the fore, and point up the difficulties that are likely to arise if the priorities of a particular group of patients differ from those of their doctors or of the wider society of which they are part. In principle, since every treatment decision entails benefits to some and disbenefits to others, in a democratic society the views of *all* affected parties should count. Since the sacrifices involved in treating particular groups of patients will be widely spread and difficult to identify with any precision, this points inexorably to the general public as the most appropriate reference group. Some people have advocated using the values of a particular reference group as the collective view (e.g. the views of the most disadvantaged, or of people with particular moral, legal or political authority). At a personal level, I feel distinctly uncomfortable about such proposals, preferring a simple populist stance. But, as I said earlier, adoption of the QALY approach does not require you to adopt this particular stance, although I must confess that it is one that I personally find very compelling.

Individual values or group values?

How should we move from individual values to group values? Once again, as a health economist, who am I to say? Once again, I don't *have* to say, because there is nothing in the QALY approach which requires aggregation to be accomplished in any particular way. But collective priority setting does require a collective view, so *some* method of aggregation has to be adopted, and whatever method is used, it will have strong ethical implications. The simplest method is to postulate that everybody's views count equally, and then take a simple average to represent the collective view. A somewhat more complicated position is involved in taking the median view as the collective view. The median view is the one that would command a simple majority in a voting system. With a skewed distribution of values (which is what is commonly found) it gives less weight to extreme views than would the taking of a simple average. But whichever position is taken on this issue, the QALY approach has the great advantage that it is not possible to hide what you have done, so it is quite easy for others to tease out the ethical implication and help ensure that you are held accountable!

Is the distribution of QALYs important?

The next set of objections to the QALY approach concentrates on whether simple maximisation of health (with all its utilitarian overtones) is really an adequate representation of social objectives in the health care field, or whether we are not also concerned with how the benefits of health care are distributed within the population. My theme here is the same as before – there is nothing in the QALY approach which requires QALYs to be used only in a maximising context, although it was QALY *maximisation* that I asked you to think about earlier as a collective prioritising rule. The use of QALYs in more complex rules is perfectly possible, and almost certainly needed if collective priority setting is to reflect the views of the general public. The simplest and commonest use of QALY calculations at present is based on the assumption that a year of healthy life expectancy is to be regarded as of equal value to every-body. Note that this does not say that it *is* of equal value to everybody, because that is unknowable. What it says is that if that social judgement is appropriate, then what follows from it will be appropriate. If it is not, then what follows will be irrelevant. A strong egalitarian case could be made for that assumption, since it implies that it does not matter at all who the beneficiary is. Like Justice, it is blind. There is no discrimination on grounds of race, sex, occupation, family circumstances, wealth or influence. In this respect it follows precisely the assumptions underlying the use of the more conventional outcome measures used in clinical trials, which just count the number of people with the specified outcome characteristic. But following hallowed tradition may not carry much weight if a sizeable majority of the general public would prefer some discrimination between potential beneficiaries according to their personal characteristics or circumstances. For instance, there is ample evidence that most people (including the elderly) would give extra weight to benefits accruing to young people over the same benefits accruing to old people. There is a similarly widespread view that people with young children should have some priority over their childless contemporaries. It is quite possible to build these differential weightings into QALY calculations, the implication being that instead of maximising *unweighted* QALYs, we would need to weigh them according to the relative priority assigned to the particular characteristics of the beneficiary. There are some espe-cially interesting issues concerning the preferential treatment of the poor. The general principle, which is widely assented to, is that access to health care should not depend on people's wealth. This implies that it should not depend on people's *lack of* wealth either! So discrimination in favour of the poor seems inconsistent. But if it is desired to use the health care system as a way of compensating people for other deprivations they suffer, then again, QALYs can be weighted accordingly.

Are there benefits other than health improvements?

Last in this group of objectors are those who assert that there are other benefits from health care than improvements in health. There obviously are. For instance, the provision of health care generates a livelihood for millions of people. Moreover, some people get satisfaction from health care in ways which do not show up as improved health. But the question is, how relevant are these other benefits for priority setting in health care? To the extent that health improvements are the dominant consideration, then QALYs, in some form or other, must be the dominant concept, on the benefit side, in collective priority setting. If the improvement of health plays only a subsidiary role, then QALYs will play only a subsidiary role. There seems little more to be said, except possibly to challenge those who reject QALYs to say what they believe the main benefits of health care are, if they are not improvements in the length and quality of people lives.

Fine in theory – but unacceptable in practice?

This brings me to my final set of people, those who accept the need for collective priority setting in principle, but are unwilling to specify how it should be done in practice. At a personal level, they have my sympathy, because of all the difficulties I have outlined. But at a professional level, I feel somewhat aggrieved by their behaviour, because a typical stance is to point out all the difficulties involved with some particular approach, and then to sit on the fence waiting for the next candidate to come by, and then do the same again. This would be fine if the implied ideal method were available to us, or if we could suspend all health care decision-making until it were. But there is no perfect system on offer, and we can't wait. As with a well-conducted clinical trial, the new has to be compared systematically, according to pre-selected criteria, with what already exists. This is what needs to happen in the field of priority setting. If the same criteria as are used to criticise the QALY approach, were used *in an even-handed way* to criticise current practice, or any feasible alternative to it, how would these *other* methods make out?

So let me end with my favourite Maurice Chevalier story. When he was getting quite old he was asked by a reporter how he viewed the ageing process. 'Well,' he said, 'there is quite a lot I don't like about it, but it's not so bad when you consider the alternative!' Perhaps the same is true of the QALY approach to collective priority setting in health care. If so, we should beware of rejecting potential improvements simply because they fall short of perfection!

NOTE

1 The interested reader may like to know that a slightly different, and fuller, version of this same argument has been published by Elsevier Science as 'QALYs and ethics: a health economist's perspective' (Alan Williams), in *Social Science and Medicine* 43, 12: 1795–804 (1996).

3

SHOULD MANAGERS ADOPT THE MEDICAL ETHIC?

Reflections on health care management[1]

Heather Draper

Relationships between clinicians and health care managers are certainly at a low ebb. Roy Lilley, whilst Chair of Homewood NHS Trust, commenting on doctors, wrote:

> when they wave the white shroud, Whitehall and most trusts seem to wave the white flag. The time has come for doctors to swap the Hippocratic Oath for something less hypocritical. . . . Recent events have shown that doctors have the power to reduce boardrooms to the level of a mad hatter's tea party. But what for? Good chairmen have been given the bullet, capable medical directors have shot themselves in the foot and talented chief executives have blown their brains out. But what has this achieved? Has it brought any patient's operation nearer, has it reassured anyone, has it brought an end to the reform of the National Health Service (NHS)? No, but it has made everyone look very foolish, selfish and inward looking.
>
> (Lilley 1994: 8)

Similarly, when clinicians were asked to comment upon managers, an empirical survey revealed some very negative responses:

38

The data . . . revealed a sense of 'apartness' between service managers and the clinicians. . . . Clinicians gave the opinion that the priority of most managers is not the welfare of patients, and that managers avoid contact with patients wherever possible . . . managers consider their main task is to achieve their fiscal objectives rather than to lead or delegate authority. The data showed significant levels of disdain for managers, and . . . anger towards them.

(Berman Brown *et al.* 1994: 67)

This chapter will explore ways in which greater trust can be gained between managers and doctors. It will be argued that it is possible for managers to be both preoccupied with the goals of management and committed to a national health service, so that the activities of clinicians and managers should not be seen as incompatible. It will also be suggested that this potential for compatibility might itself be insufficient to build bridges of trust across the professions. But, unlike Roy Lilley, who concluded that the way forward was for doctors to see their first duty as being to the organisation in which they worked, their second to their professional organisation and training, and that only then, and third, they have a duty to their patients, it will be argued that the process of rebuilding trust may require the opposite: for managers to adopt some of the values of doctors.

The above quotations have given some indication of the depth of the tension between managers and doctors but it is still useful to get a clearer view of the differences which divide the two professions.

THE DIFFERENCES BETWEEN MANAGERS AND DOCTORS

Most obvious, perhaps, is the difference in outlook. Managers typically have to deal with providing services for a whole community, whilst doctors focus on one patient at a time. Managers have, therefore, to take a broad view whilst the doctor-patient relationship tends to highlight concerns for individual interests on a one-to-one basis, and one at a time. Whilst doctors do tend to think in terms of the needs of competing existing patients, managers are often frustrated by what they perceive as doctors' total denial of opportunity costs for future patients and for patients requiring other services, perhaps from other areas of medicine. This apparent 'blindness' is perceived as a virtue by doctors whose ethical codes demand that the patient's best interests are always paramount. They argue that the caring relationship would be less effective if this were not so because the basis of the trust which a patient has in his doctor is not just that she is a competent clinician, but that she has his best interests at heart, and accordingly, she will seek only to benefit him and to avoid any unnecessary harm to him. Indeed, the obligation to the patient is such that a doctor can be held responsible for a failure of proper care or a mistake many years after the doctor-patient contact occurred, whereas managers, who work on fixed contracts, leave the responsibility for their decisions behind when they move jobs. If a doctor fails in her obligations to her patients, she may be struck off the Medical Register, losing not only her existing job, but potentially her whole livelihood. Incompetent managers may not have their contracts renewed – but this may not matter in a work climate where short contracts are the norm. Some incompetent managers are even given huge incentives to depart before their contracts expire – the managers who wasted huge amounts of money on an inadequate computer system in Birmingham are a case in point. There is little to suggest that incompetent NHS managers lose their livelihoods.

Another difference is in the professional goals of each. Doctoring tends to be something one does for life and the moral imperatives of providing good health care tend to predominate throughout, even when, at more senior levels, administration plays a larger part in daily life. Management might also be something one does for life, but health service management need not be. Indeed, for managers working in the health industry, the goals of management often seem to take precedence over the goals of health service provision. It is on this potential source of conflict that this chapter will initially concentrate.

The ideas in this chapter will be illustrated with a series of deliberately simple examples. The first is taken from the BBC *Casualty* drama. In the middle of delicate negotiations concerning the possible closure of the Holby unit, the General Manager abruptly left to take a better paid managerial post – in the tobacco industry. The message to the viewers was clear. The carers in the unit had been encouraged to have confidence in a manager who not only appeared to have had no loyalty to the existence of the unit itself but had, for reasons of self-interest, secured a post in an 'enemy' industry. The lingering question was how anyone remotely concerned about the NHS could ever work for an industry whose major side-effect is to increase ill-health in the smoking population, thereby further stretching the resources of the NHS. The manager revealed a fundamental lack of commitment to the goals and values of health care – being both willing to abandon one particular service in the midst of a crisis and to undermine the work of health care in general.

This example illustrates one of the gulfs which exist between the values of carers and those of managers. Managers often join the NHS from other industries, they may stay within the NHS only for the duration of their contract (which will typically run for a maximum of three years), they are often working on performance-related pay where performance is measured in terms of saving tax payers' money. Thus, whilst they might for the duration of their contract adopt some of the values of health provision, this is a temporary adaptation to the industry in which their skills have been employed. The values are adopted because the manager's effectiveness is measured in health care provided per pound spent. Ultimately, it is self-interest and professional pride in management skills which are the perceived sources of motivation, a perception only reinforced by the emphasis on performance-related pay in the profession. These motivations are readily transferable to other industries. Indeed, the Secretary of State for Health this year might have been the Secretary of State for Education, Defence or Agriculture and Fisheries last year. Other examples in business add weight to the argument that management skills are readily transferable – for instance the highly effective move of Graham Day from British Shipbuilders to British Leyland, or Ian McGregor's switch between British Coal and British Steel. It is difficult to see how either manager, however good at his job he was, could claim to have a vocational passion for either the preservation of shipbuilding or the coal industry. Their knowledge of shipbuilding and coal production was a means to an end rather than an end in itself. When, in 1994, Duncan Nichole joined BUPA, similar concerns were voiced about his past loyalties to the NHS.

This raises the question 'Is the same not true of health carers?'. Health carers are not condemned to work for a lifetime in the NHS; some move readily between private and public health services, others leave to become occupational doctors and nurses in industry. However, this comparison is not exact, for in such cases the essential business of preserving health and caring for patients remains.

Two further examples illustrate the difference being highlighted here between carers and managers. The first is that of a doctor who leaves the health services to become a representative for a drug company. She will certainly bring to her new career some of the knowledge acquired through her medical degree, and even some of her knowledge of health care services acquired whilst in practice. But, although her courtesy title of 'Doctor' might continue to prefix her name, she will no longer be a doctor in the sense that she was when working in the health industry. It will be an indication of her academic qualifications rather than her role, since she will no longer be 'doctoring'. A second example is the rather more extreme one of a doctor carrying out acts of torture or in some way facilitating a capital punishment, perhaps through the administration of a lethal injection. Here again, the skills of doctoring are brought to bear, but it would be outrageous to suggest one could act in such a way and remain a doctor. One cannot fly under the flag of doctor and carry out acts of torture. Even if torture, or indeed capital punishment, can be independently justified on moral grounds, no doctor may participate and remain a doctor – the clash of values inherent in each practice is too great. So whilst managers can readily move from industry to industry without any professional ethical difficulties or a significant change of professional identity, doctors clearly cannot – and I take it that the same is true for other professional carers, such as nurses.

It is clear, then, that there are certain fundamental and shared values held by those who are vocational health carers which exist beyond the skills that are required to do their jobs effectively. (Hence, it is not uncommon for health care ethics writers to observe that the expression 'the good doctor' means more than simply that the doctor is clinically competent. Clinical competence is necessary but not sufficient for one to be a good doctor.) These shared values and goals mean that whilst there is certainly rivalry between specialities and different caring roles, there is a tacit acceptance that all carers are in the same boat, paddling in the same direction. Take the situation of a single intensive care bed required by two patients, one who has had a cardiac arrest in theatre, another who has sustained multiple injuries in a car accident. In this case, the carers will negotiate for the bed from very similar positions; both will want to do the best for their patient and not wish harm to befall the other, both recognise the claim of each patient to the bed, and both trust that the other carer sincerely believes that the use of the bed is necessary for patient survival. Once the decision is taken, and provided no petty elements of rank or clinical rivalry have been permitted to muddy the waters, the 'losing' carer will probably not feel that they have been 'sold a line' or 'sold out' by the other, for the decision will have been made from a set of values and goals which both share – however frustrating both may find having to enter into such negotiations in the first place.

The question which is of interest here is whether the carers involved would feel the same way if an identical decision was made by two professional managers. Clearly, both managers would have had shared values, perhaps the impartial representation of the taxpayer through efficiency and the ultimate goal of cost reduction together with a vested self-interest in cost reduction. Indeed, with such goals, it is not impossible to imagine that each would urge the other to take the bed especially near to the end of the accounting year! Looking at things from this perspective, it is easy to see how the carers might come to believe that a management decision identical to one that they would have made for themselves is polluted, contaminated by vested self-interest and management goals, or politics, rather than a decision made in the best interests of both the patients involved. We know from other areas of health care ethics that suspicions about motive can influence our moral assessment about a decision. If a patient is going to be denied therapy, carers would expect such a decision to be made only after a good deal of soul-searching and not simply to balance the books. Good practice cannot be reduced to simple – or even quite complex – economics.

This raises the question of whether the fact that NHS management is concerned primarily with money, balancing the books and remaining in profit, or within budget, is itself an unbridgeable ethical gulf between management and doctors.

DOES PROFIT POLLUTE?

The published aim of government is to reduce NHS costs. Managers have been recruited from outside the NHS, from commerce and industry, for the specific purpose of running the NHS like any other business and on a commercial footing (Berman Brown et al. 1994: 65–6). But, as the management decision in the above example illustrated, there are those who consider that money-preoccupied motives pollute the values of providing health care within a welfare state, because doing things for profit is itself polluting. This is a view roundly rejected by Tom Sorell (Sorell and Hendry 1994: 163–73). First, he dismisses the claim that what is wrong with for-profit health care is that it is making money out of human misery. He points out that if this is wrong, then all kinds of other activities would have to be funded publicly through taxation – emergency plumbing, roofing, glazing and automobile breakdown services, for instance. Nor can it be claimed that it is because health care does not simply prevent misery but it also *saves lives* that health care cannot be provided on a for-profit basis. He argues that such a claim would not tell against placing non-life-saving activities such as some orthopaedic services on a commercial footing, but more importantly, that it is a claim which would also support a wide-scale extension of the welfare state, perhaps not to include emergency plumbing, but certainly to include many food and drugs industries.

The important moral issue, Sorell argues, is that some life-saving therapies are so expensive that they could never be provided on a commercial basis, or would not be available in all parts of the country. But this does not mean that *all* essential therapies would be necessarily dropped by a profit-motivated health service, only those which were loss-making. Moreover, in considering such therapies, a distinction must be drawn between those for-profit enterprises which are run on the *condition* that they make a profit, and those for-profit enterprises which are run only for the *sake* of profit. In the former case, it would be possible to run a health service which provided both loss- and profit-making services so long as *on balance* a profit was made. Whereas there might be good reasons to suppose that, in the latter case, any loss-making services would be axed. But there is no reason why a profit-making health service should not be run on the former 'overall profit' basis rather than on the latter 'purely for-profit' lines.

Sorell also takes a sceptical look at the force of arguments that the profit-motive produces morally superior services. We will consider only one of his arguments, the argument about waste reduction. Sorell considers wasting money (from any source, not just public funds) to be uncontroversially wrong, so that if it could be shown that a for-overall-profit health service was, by reason of being for-overall-profit, less profligate, then this might mean that it was thereby also morally superior to a non-profit-making service. Sorell rejects this claim of moral superiority on the grounds that there are plenty of examples of other non-profit-making organisations which very consciously avoid waste, and examples of 'sufficiently huge and impersonal, seemingly endlessly solvent' (Sorell and Hendry 1994: 169) private companies, where individual employees fail to take an interest in waste reduction. In the context of NHS management, these conclusions need very careful application. It would be easy to infer from Sorell's arguments (though he does not do so) that NHS management is engaged *only* in waste reduction and that this is a noble pursuit. Clearly, NHS management *is* engaged in waste reduction, and I agree with Sorell (but not for the same reasons) that this is a good thing. However, the reason that NHS management is interested in waste reduction is not because waste is bad, but because the reduction of waste is the first, most efficient, effective and least painful step towards working within the budget which is set, not by profit margins, but from on high, by central government. One of the most preoccupying roles of management in the new NHS is not the elimination of waste, but the setting of priorities. This, in practice – because of budgetary restrictions – inevitably means that some services are cut. However good the reasons are for cutting these services, these reasons are only rarely to do with waste reduction (i.e. the cutting of worthless therapy, or an expensive therapy for which a less expensive and equally effective therapy is available). More frequently, completely different therapies are assessed against one another for their relative merits. So, whilst it might not necessarily be the case that in a for-overall-profit health service expensive essential services are cut, it certainly is the case that in a service run to a fixed and limited budget such services are reduced or even axed completely.

While, then, largely agreeing with Sorell that managers simply being concerned with balancing the books or making profit is not a sufficient reason for a moral gulf between doctors and managers, I do think that a gulf is produced because managers are tied to the budgetary constraints set by central government. In fairness, it is arguable that this gulf is actually between doctors and central government. I am still optimistic, however, that it is possible for doctors and managers to be on the same side of such a gulf, provided that they share the same values.

The next perceived obstacle in the way of more harmonious relationships between doctors and managers that this chapter will address is whether it is ethically possible to place the NHS on a business footing at all.

WHAT KIND OF BUSINESS OUGHT THE NHS TO BE?

Central government encouraged the recruitment of managers from outside the NHS specifically to introduce the commercial practices of business. The emerging field of business ethics accepts that whilst there is nothing wrong with business *per se*, there can be good and bad business practices, and more and less ethical ways in which to make money. If the NHS is to be viewed as a business, what kind of business is it? And what kinds of ethical commercial practice should health care managers seek to emulate?

One of the important differences between the NHS and many other private companies is that the NHS provides a public utility in conditions of near monopoly. Of course, private hospitals exist, but they are only available to those members of the population who can afford additional insurance policies or who can pay directly for private health care. Everyone else has to rely on national insurance and the public service to which the whole working population is obliged to contribute. This element of dependence and compulsory insurance means that the NHS, unlike most other businesses, is obliged to stick to marketing the one product, health care. (Obviously the same is true of other recently privatised public utilities which hold monopolies.) Thus, there are ethical limits on the extent to which managers are free to follow their managerial instincts to diversify into other markets, and these limits are set by the obligation to provide a public health service (for more on this, see Draper 1996).

It is folly to think that NHS management has not attempted to diversify into other areas of commerce and, it must be said, it has done so within ethically acceptable limits, despite the views of those for whom this diversification is perceived as another mark of a fundamental clash of values. In the hospitals of the new NHS, public areas are generously bestowed with a variety of shops; the catering divisions may tender for outside catering contracts and offer limited outside catering services; and the linen departments may offer a commercial dry cleaning service to employees. One hospital in the East Midlands has built a hotel over its maternity unit. Indeed, management may even be willing to sell its own managerial and computing expertise to other NHS Trusts. All these activities raise money which is then ploughed back into the main business of providing health care. The ethical limit which has to be placed on this diversification is that the business of providing the best possible health care remains the central and primary one. However much more profit would be made by so doing, managers could never simply close down the health care activities of the sole hospital in an area and turn it into a hotel run on a profitable basis. Clearly, this is an extreme and obvious example but it echoes the worries of carers whose mistrust in management is so great that they believe that managers would, if given the choice, run hospitals with as few patients as possible in order to balance the books. Cancelling theatre lists and temporarily closing wards is, after all, a common and immediately effective method of saving money and remaining within budget.

Whatever managers (or others) think that they are doing, ethical business practice dictates that NHS managers are dedicated to the provision of health care. But part of the problem between doctors and managers is that the managers themselves and their spokespersons are prepared to allow this message to be oblique. Consider the following extract: 'In striving to meet Government's objectives, even for purely selfish reasons, the managers will, by definition, be putting the interests of patients first. In other words, the Government philosophy is simply a variation of Adam Smith's 'hidden hand' (Berman Brown *et al.* 1994: 66).

Perhaps one of the fundamental differences between NHS managers and doctors is that doctors believe they have a specific duty to their patients, whereas for managers it is apparently enough that patient welfare is a means – albeit a vital means – through which other ends are achieved. But managers could alter this emphasis within the context of their own professional ethics and good business practice, and in so doing they would take an important step towards reconciliation with carers. It is for this reason that managers need to adopt the medical ethic. This will go a long way to building up trust because it makes explicit a commitment to the health service in the form of the NHS and to patient care, and in so doing places carers and managers firmly on the same side.

So what would the decisions of the doctor-thinking managers be like. This is the subject of the final part of the chapter.

THE DOCTOR-THINKING MANAGER

Interestingly, encouraging this ethos of managers thinking in part like carers has some less obvious results, which can be illustrated by looking at some further decisions about resource allocation.

Consider this example taken from the BBC Radio 4 programme *Doctors*, set in a fundholding general practice. Fundholders have considerable discretion over how to spend surpluses in their budget. One GP in *Doctors* wanted to provide some nicotine patches to enable a patient to quit smoking. Nicotine patches and chewing gum are now available over the counter without prescription, whereas previously, although the patient had to pay the retail price for the drug, it could only be obtained via prescription. This GP wanted the practice to pay for the patches on behalf of the patient who, she believed, was too poor to buy them himself. The decision was clear-cut for the GP concerned. The patient wanted to give up smoking which was proving harmful to his health. The GP, concerned for the patient's best health interests, felt that this was a legitimate expenditure of the practice's surplus health care budget. What might a manager, thinking in part like a doctor, have decided here?

In thinking like a doctor, the manager would certainly have recognised the desirability of the prescription. But she would ultimately have decided against the subsidised provision of the drugs for the following reasons. First, whilst the doctor was responding as one who *cares*, she was not thereby necessarily responding as a *health* carer since the financial aspect of the decision was motivated by the patient's perceived poverty rather than his health status. It is not surprising that doctors respond in this way, since most are genuinely concerned about their patients. But the link with health care in this case is tenuous, despite the fact that, if successful, the prescription may save money for the NHS in the future. This is precisely where managers have a duty to act not only with reference to the business of providing health care, but also as the impartial guardians of the tax-payers' money. Rightly or wrongly, the NHS budget is restricted to health, not social services, and it would therefore be inappropriate to spend the money from one budget when it possibly needs to come from the other. Moreover, saving money from being diverted down this different, though related, channel actually conforms with the goals which both doctor and doctor-thinking manager share, which is the best possible provision of health care. Responding simply as someone who cares, perhaps it would have been appropriate for the doctor to have considered dipping into her own pocket where the competing obligations of her different caring roles – perhaps as both doctor and provider for a family – might then have appeared more obvious to her. The manager's distance from the patient might enable her to ask two distinct questions: 'Is this just a *caring* thing to do?' or 'Is it a *health care* activity?' Second, the argument about poverty does not work all that well either, since patches and gum are priced in much the same range (not surprisingly) as cigarettes. Thus, one way of helping the patient to afford the prescription might have been to have split the patch packet and sold it in units of pence more directly reflecting the price of cigarettes, which are often bought one packet at a time rather than in bulk, especially by those whose budgets do not permit bulk-buy savings.

Another complaint about managers is that they never have to live with the effects of their decisions – namely, to be the one telling the patient: 'No, we cannot give you this treatment.' This insulation from individual suffering, it is claimed, inclines managers to be callous and uncaring. Discussion of the role of the doctor-thinking manager using the following example might help to dispel this view too.

A decision has been taken by a local NHS Trust to limit the numbers of expensive heart-lung transplantation operations by putting a ceiling on expenditure. Just as the money runs out, the press begins to highlight the plight of a child who will be refused an operation as a result. It is unlikely that the child will survive into the next financial year. At first the press question the paediatrician who leaves them in no doubt that responsibility for the decision must be laid at the door of the managers who determined the division of funding. Faced with a storm of bad publicity and political pressure, the chief executive of the Trust decides to use money from a contingency fund to buy the child's operation at a national specialist hospital currently offering the best value for money for this procedure.

This *appears* to be an example of how a manager has responded like a carer: when faced with an identifiable individual he found it impossible not to care about the suffering which one of his policy decisions might generate. Nevertheless, in the spirit of management, he shopped around for the best deal. But is this *really* a case of acting from common values? In the first place, since the decision was influenced by the risk of bad publicity and possible legal and political repercussions, it only reflects skilful management, not doctor-thinking management (even taking into account that standard clinical practice is becoming more defensive). Moreover, this example illustrates a further source of mistrust felt by carers, who do see decisions such as this as one of prudence rather than concern, and also feel aggrieved that managers do not stick to the guns of a policy decision when it is they, rather than the carers, who are in the firing line. In the second place, this decision may not have actually promoted the values of health caring, because it has diverted money away from others who require help but whose cases are less newsworthy. Carers are supposed to be impartial and are expected to treat all their patients equally, with regard only for their needs rather than their newsworthiness. Thus, it is highly likely that a doctor-thinking manager would *not* have financed the operation because to do so would not have promoted health care impartially within his realm of influence. If anything, the situation is more akin to the GP and the nicotine patch. There is a very human desire to help those in distress – especially when faced with a direct and personal appeal – but this help cannot always be provided from the current NHS budget if justice is to be done to the legitimate claims of other users.

In thinking like a doctor, the health care manager has to acquire some of the clinician's single-minded dedication to his patient group, rather than to the whim of public interest (the pressure from which must be almost irresistible when individual cases, particularly those involving children, are highlighted). Government policy has, to some extent, hampered such single-minded dedication by insisting that commissioners consult their local population about the sort of health care services it wants (Department of Health 1989). Yet the views of the population may not coincide with effective commissioning and may, therefore, undermine both effective service provision and distributive justice (Draper and Tunna 1996: 4–5).

The final example is of a doctor who wants to prescribe an expensive but potentially life-saving drug regime for a patient. The patient will certainly die without it and may survive if it is given. However, the expense will cut deep into the budget allocated for the unit to the detriment of future patients. The doctor realises this, but believing that he must act in the best interests of this patient – and after all tomorrow is another day – decides to go ahead and initiate the treatment. What would the doctor-thinking manager's response to this situation have been? Undoubtedly, she would consider this to fall within the remit of health care – unlike, perhaps, the financing of the nicotine patch. However, because of her broader perspective she would see herself as having a much stronger duty to future patients because providing an overall service in the best interest of all potential patients is her primary concern. She would, though, as a doctor-thinking manager be acutely aware of the dynamics of the doctor-patient relationship in which the patient's trust that the doctor is always on his side is vital. Thus, she would see that it is impossible for the doctor to deny the patient this treatment and will shoulder the responsibility for denying it herself as this is the best means of promoting the values of health care in this situation.

This suggestion that a manager should interfere in the clinical decision of a doctor will rankle with many doctors who will wish to assert that clinical freedom should be absolute. There is, however, a good *clinical* precedent for this sort of division of management of patients which can be seen in operation in GPs' referrals to hospital consultants – though in this case it is a matter of custom rather than design. Prior to fundholding, a GP referred any patients she thought in need of hospital care to the appropriate consultant. The patient was assessed by the consultant, who then decided what treatment, if any, would be given. As a consequence, if the consultant refused therapy (on the grounds of cost or age or smoking habits, etc.) the GP's relationship with the patient was preserved. One of the perceived advantages of the fundholding system is that it gives GPs greater control over their budgets. However, it is now the GP who has to decide whether or not to refer for tertiary care, according to their own practice's budget, i.e. the GP is making the initial assessments based on cost, age and habits that were previously made by a consultant. This will undoubtedly have a negative effect on the doctor-patient relationship. When a GP denies her patient the therapy he needs, to whom does the patient then turn? Would he trust her to provide him with adequate palliative care at home when she appears to have denied him the opportunity of cure in hospital? In the NHS, the GP is not just the gatekeeper to tertiary services, she is also the first, continuing and last port of call for patients, the person who must always be available and whose duty it is to care when all other services fail. Even the most demanding/undesirable patients are not abandoned by the GP system, being allocated by the FHSA to local practices in rotation. This does not mean that the GP can always do much more than listen and sympathise, but she cannot deprive a patient of care. Unless she is a fundholder – or so the warnings read. Clearly, once financial considerations come into the GP's decision to refer, the patient's trust in the relationship may be eroded.

And so it may also be with consultants, to return to our example, who have to provide long-term more holistic in-patient care as well as out-patient short-term consultations. One role for doctor-thinking managers in allocating decisions is to be overtly seen to carry the can so that the caring relationship can remain insulated from the economic realities in which it is forced to work. The suggestion here is that the manager is to the consultant as the consultant is to the GP. This is not a matter of spending more or less, but focusing the responsibilities differently within the service. This may go some way to addressing the criticism made by doctors of managers that was cited at the beginning of the chapter: i.e. that managers are apart and do not take responsibilities or a lead in decision-making. It does not mean that doctors lose their clinical autonomy, as they will remain free to recommend first options and second options if the first options are refused by management. Likewise, they will still have to determine whether a therapy will *benefit* a patient at all or whether the *burden* of the therapy *outweighs* the *benefit* – the kinds of decisions which are often required at the end of life and for which management skills are entirely unsuited. However, the economic implication of these decisions are immense, as any scan through the recent literature on withdrawing life-prolonging therapy will show. Decisions about effective therapy will always require clinical judgement and this is one area where cooperation between managers and carers would be hugely beneficial.

The public had a glimpse of the potential benefits of this kind of partnership in January 1995, when Cambridge and Huntingdon Health Authority decided to withhold further treatment from a ten-year-old child with myeloid leukaemia. Jaymee Bowen had received aggressive therapy for five years, but when she relapsed following a bone marrow transplant from her sister, the Authority decided that the potential health gain was not sufficient to justify further intervention. Jaymee's doctors only rated the chances of success at around 2 per cent for two years. Despite huge public interest and a protracted legal battle, the authority stuck to its decision, although the child was subsequently treated (with a different therapy) at a private hospital after an anonymous donor intervened with £75,000.

There is one significant difference between Jaymee's case and the previous example. Jaymee's doctors believed that further intervention was not in *her* best interests: the cost to her in terms of pain and suffering would not be outweighed by the small chance of some additional life. The attractive feature of the case, from the point of view of this chapter, was that the management made it quite clear that it was they who were refusing to fund the therapy, they took total responsibility for making this decision in the light of clinical (and ethical) advice from Jaymee's doctors, and they refused to capitulate even under the adverse glare of the media.

CONCLUSION

Undoubtedly, relationships between managers and doctors – and indeed other practitioners – are strained. Managers from industry and commerce were encouraged to enter the NHS to place it on a business footing. Practitioners, often ideologically opposed to reform, have distrusted managers, believing that the NHS should be focused on patient care and not finances (even though the two are not mutually exclusive). Even when clinicians have accepted that reforms may indeed benefit patients, managers have still been viewed as 'the enemy'. One notable exception has been the employment of practice managers by fundholding GPs. In this case, GPs have embraced the benefits of having a qualified person to sort out the maze of claims and contracts upon which their incomes depend. The significant difference between managers in general practice and managers in hospital is that the GPs employ the managers and therefore feel in control of the management decisions which are made. They are also active in decisions about how their (now dwindling) surpluses are to be spent. In hospitals, even when a manager is employed from within the NHS, recruited from the ranks of the clinicians themselves, they are perceived by all practitioners as having 'gone over to the other side'.

Managers could do more to improve their relationships with clinicians, which have to be built on mutual trust. Managers have to trust practitioners' judgements about the benefits and effectiveness of therapy but, for such a partnership to be launched, practitioners have to trust the motives of the managers. It has been shown in this chapter that benefiting patients should be the primary goal of managers because the business to which the NHS is dedicated is the business of providing health care. They differ from practitioners, perhaps, in that managers see patient care as a valuable means to an end rather than as an end in itself. What is less clear is whether managers have a commitment to the NHS as the best medium for providing health care; some do not even have a commitment to health care *per se*, being happy to move from one management environment to another. If managers were able to convince all practitioners – not just doctors – that they were committed to caring for patients within the NHS, this would provide the foundation for improved relationships. It remains with managers to make the first move here, not only because effective management builds up good staff relationships, but also because the managers are largely forced upon the carers rather than chosen by them.

Perhaps the best gesture of goodwill is for all health care management within the NHS to be viewed as a vocation, with managers for the NHS being trained within the NHS, rather than being brought in from business and commerce with little knowledge of health care. There is no reason why health managers cannot become another profession allied to medicine, with its own professional ethical codes and standards of practice which reflect a primary goal of patient care within the NHS. As managers, they would have a responsibility for the most prudent use of NHS resources, but rather than financial incentives, they would be influenced by the same incentives as practitioners – the satisfaction of patient care as the carrot and the threat of removal from the professional register as the stick. This latter incentive would make managers more accountable for their actions over the whole of their careers rather than simply for the duration of their contracts. Likewise, managers could have security of contract within which to develop services. Reinforcing the shared goals of practitioners and management should go some way to building the mutual respect between the professions.

The most important management objective of recent times has been to determine health care priorities – rationing by another name. This activity, if it is to be at all ethical, has to be based on some understanding of effective medicine: outcomes of care rather than just processes of care. Managers need clinicians to execute and interpret clinical audits in order to determine where health care resources can best be spent. Lack of data about the effectiveness of many medical practices has made contracting on the basis of cost-effectiveness almost impossible (Maynard 1994: 1439). To purchase and provide effectively, managers need the cooperation of all practitioners. Cooperation requires trust and the onus lies with the managers to win this trust by incorporating within their business ethic some of the ethical principles of health care. Roy Lilley wrote that the first duty of doctors is to the organisation within which they work. By organisation he undoubtedly meant local Trusts. Ironically, doctors do have a huge institutional loyalty, but this loyalty is not to the commercial aspects of the NHS but to the 'business' of providing health care. It is this commitment to the business of providing health care which has the potential to unite practitioners and management.

NOTE

1 Since this paper was presented at 'Rationing Health Care' (Middlesex University, September 1994), there have been several changes, for instance in government and therefore government policy, and in the training of health service managers. The new Labour Government announced in December 1997 its intention to phase out fundholding and also to unify some parts of the health and social services budgets.

BIBLIOGRAPHY

Berman Brown, R., Bell, L. and Scaggs, S. (1994) 'Who is the NHS for?', *Journal of Management in Medicine* 8, 4: 62–70.

Department of Health (1989) *Working for Patients*, Cmnd 555, London: HMSO.

Draper, H. (1996) 'Can Britain's NHS managers be business-like and should they adopt the values of business?', *Business Ethics: A European Review* 5, 4: 207–11.

Draper, H. and Tunna, K. (1996) *Ethics and Values for Commissioners*, Leeds: Nuffield Institute for Health.

Lilley, R. (1994) 'Viewpoint', *HealthCare Today* Nov./Dec.: 8.

Maynard, A. (1994) 'Can Competition enhance efficiency in health care?: lessons from the reform of the UK National Health Service', *Social Science and Medicine* 39, 10: 1433–45.

Sorell, T. and Hendry, J. (1994) *Business Ethics*, Oxford: Butterworth-Heinemann.

4

MANAGEMENT, ETHICS AND THE ALLOCATION OF RESOURCES

Ruth Chadwick

Health service managers have a responsibility to use resources responsibly (Ashcroft 1996). To say that managers should use resources 'responsibly' however tells us too little. What counts as responsible use? Presumably it implies at least that wastefulness should be avoided, but it does not signify anything about the criteria of distribution to be employed, in terms of effectiveness, efficiency or fairness. As one Chief Executive has pointed out, 'Each health authority will adopt its own methodology for allocating priorities and listen to a range of individuals and local organisations' (Ashcroft 1996: 4).

The question of criteria of distribution of health resources has received much attention from health economists, philosophers, health professionals and public policy-makers, but remains a contested area. This is partly because central concepts in the debate, such as 'justice' and 'equity' are themselves contested concepts. But there is also confusion because of the various levels at which decisions are and should be taken. Managers, in particular, are subject to competing demands, for example to respect budgets, to consult the public, to abide by the stated values of the service, whether they should become involved with individual cases or only with making decisions about services.

A 'MANAGEMENT' PERSPECTIVE?

We first have to be clear about what is meant by 'management' in this context. What I am concerned with is the management task of taking decisions about commissioning and possibly disinvesting in services. The class of people responsible for this may be subject to change, for example as a result of government policy regarding the National Health Service (NHS), but the task of setting priorities remains. Some of these decision-makers may in fact be clinicians, but will be taking resource allocation decisions not *qua* clinicians, but wearing a management hat. Thus it is the activity rather than particular persons that is under discussion.

Chambers defines the manager as 'one who organises other people's doings'. If those people's doings were not worthwhile, the activity of the manager, similarly, would be worthless. Management has no intrinsic value of its own: it has only instrumental value, in so far as it contributes to the goals of the activity in question. Interesting questions arise in the discussion of what those goals are and/or should be. We cannot assume that the ethical manager is simply one who adopts morally acceptable means to achieve goals. Aristotle distinguished between mere cleverness, which is being good at working out ways to achieve objectives, and practical wisdom, which involves also seeing what the right ends are. He was making the point that there is a moral question to be asked about goals. In the present context it has been suggested that too little effort has been devoted to what the objectives of the health care system should be: 'You must first of all pick your social ethic. Only after you have done that can you discuss efficiency at all' (Uwe Reinhardt, quoted in Office of Health Economics 1997).

In practice, however, there is a question about the extent to which managers do or can consider questions of social ethics. Evidence suggests that decisions on, for example, disinvestment in existing service provision are likely to be guided not by the explicit choice of a social ethic so much as by the likelihood of political, public or pressure group resistance, or by the costly consequences in terms of unused plant and staff (Working Party on Priority Setting 1998). In the light of this, certain tactics, such as the use of waiting lists and transfer of responsibility to other services, for example social services, have proved popular, while commissioning agencies have nevertheless expressed interest in guidance on the principles to be invoked, especially with new developments and technologies (*ibid.*).

A good place to start in thinking about applicable principles for managers working in the NHS is to consider the goals of that service. Despite the frequently made comment that the NHS is in reality an illness service rather than a health service, the goals to be considered must have something to do with health. But is it possible to be more specific? There is a question here about what the goals *are*, as determined by the government of the day, and what they *should* be. The latter provides an area for dispute between a community-centred and an individual-centred approach.

THE GOALS OF THE NHS

Anthony Culyer (1997) has argued that a principal objective of the NHS is maximising the health of the whole community. Maximising is about efficiency, not effectiveness. Effectiveness, says Culyer, differs from efficiency in taking no account of opportunity cost. Culyer acknowledges the is/ought dichotomy and says that a principal objective of the NHS *is* maximising the health of the whole community because there is ministerial authority for this. He also states that it *ought* to be a principal objective of the NHS on the basis of the following argument:

1 Flourishing is an ultimate good.
2 Good health is (in general) a necessary condition of flourishing.
3 Health care may be necessary (though not sufficient) for realising better health.

In point 2 the aim of the words in parenthesis is to acknowledge the exceptional cases of those who flourish despite what might be considerable degrees of ill health. In point 3, while it is clear that health care is not a sufficient condition of better health, given the number of determinants of health, it is also not possible to state that it is necessary, though in some circumstances it may be.

John Harris (1997) argues against this point of view on the grounds that maximising the health of the *whole* community may have the effect of systematically advantaging some sections of the community. For example, he says, if all seriously ill people were allowed to die, this might dramatically improve aggregate health. What should be the case is that each individual has an equal chance of flourishing. This implies that what the objective of the NHS should be (irrespective of what it actually is at any given time) is to offer beneficial health care on the basis of individual need.

There seems to be some agreement here on the idea that the objective of the NHS is to offer health care as a means to the promotion of flourishing, but there is disagreement as to whether this flourishing should be maximised over the whole community or whether the individual ought to be at the centre of decision-making.

What I want to suggest is that there are certain concepts used freely in the debate which are susceptible of different interpretation according to which of these approaches is taken; and that the actual policies of the day have a tendency to exploit these ambiguities. The manager's position is then very unclear. The value of ethical theory is not so much that it provides a source of guidance as to the 'right answers' in determining what the objectives of the NHS ought to be and, in the light of that, what services ought to be prioritised. It is rather that it sheds light on what actually is being demanded of management within a given system.

INDIVIDUALISM

What factors might be involved in an individual-centred approach to management decision-making? Certainly in the context of clinical decision-making there is a widespread perception that medical ethics is primarily about promoting the interest of the individual patient (and hence that 'priority setting' or 'rationing' is not an option) whether or not this is interpreted in terms of beneficence, non-maleficence, or autonomy. The fact that justice is the fourth of the 'four principles' approach, now very popular in biomedical ethics, perhaps to a certain extent acknowledges the competing claims of different patients. But there is still support for another principle, not one of the four, viz. the principle of rescue – that we should do all we can to save the individual life. The fact that there is strong intuitive support for this principle is apparent from the powerful effects of media presentations of individual cases, however irrational it may be that people are moved more by the one identifiable case than the deaths of a larger number of 'anonymous' people.

It has already been pointed out that managers are not making decisions in a clinical capacity, and although they may sometimes become involved in individual cases, we are primarily concerned with prioritising services. A decision about the latter, however, can sometimes lead to the well-publicised individual case where 'rescue' is pitted against the management decision. The principle of rescue is however only practicable when applied to a select number of (often very highly publicised) cases. It is increasingly recognised that it would not be feasible to 'do everything' to save every individual, although, on the other hand, it continues to be held that NHS funding is sufficient (Light 1997). The NHS White Paper (1997), acknowledging rising public expectations, says that they 'should be channelled into shaping services to make them more responsive to the needs and preferences of the people who use them' (1997: 7–8). It rejects the suggestion that the arguments in favour of rationing or charging are convincing. It is also committed to ending unfairness (1997: 13).

In such a situation, in what ways is it possible for the manager to adopt an ethical perspective, to strike a course between meeting demand and avoiding unfairness? Departing from the principle of rescue, the manager might turn to ways of assessing claims for resources on the basis of certain criteria of what is fair and just.

JUSTICE

The view that allocation should be according to need is a conception of justice that has a long tradition of support in the context of the provision of health services. The Dutch Health Council in its report *Choices in Health Care*, however, demonstrated very well how different actors in the debate have different perspectives on the concept of need. From the point of view of the individual, they suggested, individual goals determine need; the professionals (providers) argue for need as objectively determined by biomedical limitations; from the point of view of the community, however, inability to participate in society determines need (Health Council of The Netherlands 1992: 50). This suggests that a manager could put need at the centre of decision-making, but that he or she is unlikely to interpret it as a clinician might. So with respect to the question whether need counts as an individual-centred approach, there is an ambiguity over whether that is because the criterion used involves need as interpreted by the individual or the need *of* the individual as interpreted by someone else. 'Need' could also be part of a community-based approach. The NHS White Paper, in the statement that 'In the new NHS patients will be treated according to need and need alone' (1997: 13), is able to exploit this ambiguity.

There are, however, reasons why a manager might not want to use need as the primary factor in decision-making about resources. One is that it does not follow from the fact that we have identified needs (however that is done) that the resources are there to satisfy them. The second report of the Working Party on Priority Setting finds evidence of reluctance to discover unmet and unmeetable

needs (1998). It may still be necessary to prioritise between identified needs, unless we allow resource availability to have an influence
in determining how we interpret the concept of need, which is to
approach the issue from the wrong direction.

In such a situation a manager might turn to utilitarianism – in
fact it might be suggested that a manager who is responsible for
purchasing services for substantial sections of the population is
bound to employ some version of utilitarianism. Utilitarianism
includes both a concept of utility and a principle of maximisation.
In other words, there is some conception of what counts as success,
and a principle that we should have as much of it as possible. In the
context of health care, what should this be? One of the attractions
of the Quality Adjusted Life Year (QALY) was that it provided the
possibility of both a clear and a numerical measure of success.
Criticisms of it have been widespread, partly on the grounds that, as
originally formulated, it took no account of equity in distribution.
Work now centres on ways of factoring equity into outcome
measures, but Culyer points out that equity may not be sufficiently
served by maximising an equity-weighted outcome measure (1997).
Also important is the attempt to move towards some equal distribution of health across the population as a whole. So maximising
health for the community in some kind of utilitarian way may not
be sufficient, although a measure of outcome born from this type of
reasoning may be a valuable tool for the manager.

One criticism of utilitarian thinking of a fairly crude sort is that
it is prepared to sacrifice the interests of individuals in the course of
its maximising policy. This is part of the reason for public outrage
at the stories of individuals in great distress who are apparently
denied the treatment they need to survive. From another perspective
utilitarianism itself can still be seen as an approach which puts the
individual at the centre of decision-making. As Derek Parfit has put
it, 'Each counts for one. That is why more count for more' (Parfit
1978: 301). Each person, or each person's equal interest, has equal
weight. Ironically, the Working Party on Priority Setting finds few
attempts to use utilitarian-type outcome measures for overall policy,
such as ranking of services, though such measures might be used to
assess an appropriate response in a particular individual case.

In thinking about individual cases, however, a complicating
factor is the influence of the meritorian or desert conception of
justice, which holds that what is fair is that individuals should be
treated according to what they deserve. This leads to considerable

controversy in the health care context, on several different grounds. First, it might be argued that health care is the kind of good for which this kind of criterion is inappropriate; second, that it is unworkable, because it is doubtful that many of us could claim to be blameless; third, that health professionals should be making decisions on the basis of medical evidence and not on the grounds of moral desert. On the other hand, in Germany it has been argued that 'personal responsibility, not rationing, is the way forward', because rationing is too politically sensitive *(BMJ* 1997), while in The Netherlands it has been suggested that, although it is morally acceptable to encourage personal responsibility, responsibility cannot be used as a criterion in allocating treatment (Health Council of The Netherlands 1992).

Contest in this area takes place over whether certain sorts of judgement are *actually* made on the basis of moral or medical criteria. For example, a case reported in the *BMJ* described a girl denied a kidney transplant allegedly on the grounds of bad school behaviour and use of ecstasy (Dyer 1997). Her mother also had a history of drug misuse. The surgeon in question, however, defended her decision on medical grounds – namely that the chances of success were very low.

How might these considerations inform decisions about services rather than individuals? There could be a policy in a region that smokers will not be allocated certain kinds of treatment. Under one interpretation this can be viewed as a judgement on the moral responsibility of smokers. From another point of view it is an estimate of likely outcomes. In practice, of course, it is very unlikely that the grounds for a decision of this type can be isolated.

It is clear from this discussion that even if the stated goals of the service are to meet the needs of individuals, and that this is what they ought to be, there is scope for different interpretations. Moreover, it is desirable to have some way of prioritising between identified needs, which leads to consideration of competing conceptions of justice.

THE COMMUNITY APPROACH

If we turn to the view that the goals of the service are and should be concerned with the health of the community, the idea of need will be differently perceived. Although the NHS White Paper puts together the idea of tailoring the services to the needs of individual patients with that of making them 'more responsive to the needs and preferences of the people who use them', the latter idea would not be incompatible, under some interpretations, with a community-based approach. Henk ten Have has pointed out that a communitarian perspective, although liable to be mistakenly identified with a utilitarian approach, is not in essence utilitarian. On the contrary, it is dependent on a 'normative, deontological framework defining the meaning of community interests' (ten Have 1993: 45). From this perspective values are not dependent upon individual interests, wants or needs but come from the community:

> the moral agent should not be viewed in an atomistic way, but rather as situated in a moral community from which he derives his moral identity, his substantial moral convictions and his sense of direction. The moral community provides the individual with a moral space within which he inevitably finds himself located, and from which he derives the resources by means of which moral problem situations can be evaluated.
>
> (Zwart 1993: 53–4)

So values are derived from practices and ways of living. When the community is the centre of decision-making, the responsibilities, rather than the rights, of the individual may be emphasised. The very sense of what is beneficial to the individual is likely to be different than according to an individualistic perspective.

What follows for the manager from this point of view? He or she has to try to determine what the values of the community are – to elucidate a communitarian consensus. The possibility of doing this is subject to the criticism that it is theoretically impossible in contemporary society.

> The dominant forms of public life – the market, bureaucracy, are incompatible with community in this sense. Those who have involved the concept against liberalism have simply evaded the central problem which liberalism is attempting to confront – the place of values in a value-free world.
>
> (Poole 1991: 88)

Zwart has argued that the liberal-communitarian opposition can be understood in terms of two different points of view: the willingness to intervene and the willingness to accept. From the liberal viewpoint we are willing to intervene, to do what we can to save the individual – hence the intuitive support for the principle of rescue. From the communitarian perspective we are willing to accept that we cannot do everything. This is slightly misleading, however, because in the second alternative it is a very different matter to be in the position of the one who decides that he or she cannot offer help from being in the position of the individual who will not receive the help desired or needed. So there is an opposition both between the attitudes of the decision-makers and between the status of the potential patients in the two perspectives.

So the communitarian manager has to accept that there are limits, but seeks to elucidate the communitarian consensus on values to aid him or her in making allocation decisions. This, I suggest, is in accord with the contemporary trend towards consulting the public on rationing or priority setting, by citizens' juries and the like. Of course, in the light of Poole's points, a danger is that what might be gained is not a communitarian consensus but a utilitarian majority vote. But this is perhaps too pessimistic. Although consensus in contemporary society may not be readily available, it might be a mistake to think that it cannot be constructed (cf. Moon 1993) via consensus conferences, for example, provided that sufficient safeguards are put in place to minimise the risk of excluding less powerful voices from the process. Culyer argues that equity concerns are not exhausted by equity in distribution: procedures and processes too must be fair. The sorts of procedures he appears to have in mind include waiting times, but they should also include means of constructing consensus.

While consulting the public will be important in carrying out the responsibility of facilitating health care for the local population, Len Doyal and Ian Gough have a worry about the communitarian project carried out at local level:

> any local, community-based, small-scale form of need satisfaction can foster 'insider' conceptions of human need and inhibit the growth of generalisable notions based on a wider collective identity. . . . The dream of a community politics which could unite different groups . . . cannot be realised in the absence of precisely such a cross-cultural and cross-group source of identity as human need.
>
> (Doyal and Gough 1991: 308–9)

What this section has shown is that the goals of meeting needs and consulting the public could be compatible with a communitarian approach rather than an individual-centred approach. The manager here in consulting the public would not be eliciting consumer preferences but elucidating a *consensus*.

AN ALTERNATIVE APPROACH: TWO TIERS AND VIRTUE ETHICS

Before drawing any conclusion about this debate it is worth noting a different trend in this context which would put yet another slant on the manager's consultation role. The NHS White Paper expresses support for universalism but there is a view that in Europe there is an inevitable move towards 'two-tier' health care systems – a basic package and supplementary systems. Sass has argued that in the old way of viewing health care systems, solidarity was appropriate as a principle (Sass 1995). In the new model, a triad of principles has taken its place: self-responsibility, solidarity and subsidiarity. At the level of the basic package, solidarity with those in need and distributive justice remain appropriate.

Beyond that, subsidiarity suggests that 'whatever the individual can do, should not be done by the state or by social institutions or uniform services'. This facilitates the notion of personal responsibility. Responsibility here should not be understood, however, in terms of the desert model of justice, but in terms of virtue ethics. According to Sass, in the old system, 'a patient's moral virtues were seen as limited mainly to compliance and hope'. In the new system, the patient is to be encouraged to an attitude of acceptance and to being responsible. This 'encouragement' would presumably require programmes of public awareness and reflection on what it is reasonable to expect health care to provide (Sass 1995).

How could the management perspective fit into this approach? Reinhardt has suggested a system where there could be a single-tier system funded from taxation, but an option to buy extra care, with the possibility of choosing between competing purchasers, based initially on current district health authorities. It would then be incumbent on these purchasers to give high quality information to potential clients, in addition to their obligation to manage the publicly funded service.

In a different context, the provision of information is recognised as an important objective by Culyer: 'improved health is not the only business of the NHS. In relations with patients a common task in both primary and secondary care is to provide information – and no more' (1997). It is certainly the case that in some services, genetics services for example, the outcome aimed at may be more informed clients, rather than health gain as identified by some outcome measure, for example the QALY. In fact it has been a feature of genetics services that they have sought to distance themselves from objectives in terms of the health of the population. It is important therefore, for a number of reasons, that managers take on board the informational aspect of their role, in addition to maximising the health of the community or promoting the flourishing of the individuals within their sphere of influence.

CONCLUSION

Managers may have strategies, such as the use of waiting lists, to help them in allocating resources, but there is also an issue about ethical criteria in allocation. It is therefore useful to explore what ethical theory has to offer. Managers, however, have to take decisions within a number of constraints, the most obvious being the goals of the service as defined by the government of the day. These may be subject to change, but the concepts employed allow for varying interpretation under different ethical perspectives. The values inherent in the service (cf. Working Party on Priority Setting 1996: 11–12) have been stated to be equity, efficiency and responsiveness (developed into the principles of equity, public choice and effective use of resources), which seem under one interpretation to represent an attempt to negotiate between individual and community. Equity, although the meaning is contested, aims at a fair distribution between individuals as well as seeking to narrow the gap between the better and worse off. Efficiency pays regard to outcomes. Responsiveness is the value that reflects the importance assigned to consulting the population, which seems to be in accordance with the idea of establishing a consensus.

The White Paper, however, appears to be attempting to reinforce the importance of an individual-centred approach. In the light of this, it is necessary to consider what is the objective in consulting the public. It could be a way of establishing a community consensus, eliciting consumer preferences, or it could have an educative role. Thus, although the ethical manager operates within constraints in terms of stated goals, he or she has scope for various interpretations. This is where the role of management overlaps with the discussion of what the goals of the health service *should* be, and this, rather than answering specific priority setting questions, is where ethical theory has a role to play.

BIBLIOGRAPHY

Ashcroft, S. (1996) 'The moral maze – organisational ethics within NHS Trusts', *Professional Opinion* 2, Preston: Centre for Professional Ethics.

British Medical Journal (1997) 'Personal responsibility, not rationing, is the way forward', *British Medical Journal* 314: 1712.

Culyer, A. J. (1997) 'Maximising the health of the whole community', British Medical Journal 314: 667–9.

Doyal, L. and Gough, I. (1991) *A Theory of Human Need*, Houndmills: Macmillan.

Dyer, C. (1997) 'Doctors accused of refusing transplant on moral grounds', *British Medical Journal* 314: 1370.

Harris, J (1997) 'The case against [Culyer]', *British Medical Journal* 314: 669–72.

Health Council of The Netherlands (1992) *Choices in Health Care: A Report by the Government Committee on Choices in Health Care*, A. J. Dunning (Chairman), Rijswijk: Ministry of Health, Welfare and Cultural Affairs.

Light, D. W. (1997) 'The real ethics of rationing', *British Medical Journal* 315: 112–5.

Moon, J. D. (1993) *Constructing Community: Moral Pluralism and Tragic Conflicts*, Princeton: Princeton University Press.

Office of Health Economics (1997) *OHE News* 5: 1–3.

Parfit, D.(1978) 'Innumerate ethics', *Philosophy and Public Affairs* 7, 4: 285–301.

Poole, R. (1991) *Morality and Modernity*, London: Routledge.

Sass, H-M. (1995) 'The new triad: responsibility, solidarity and subsidiarity', *Journal of Medicine and Philosophy* 20, 6: 587–94.

ten Have, H. A. M. J. (1993) 'Choosing core services in the Netherlands', *Health Care Analysis* 1, 1: 43–7.

White Paper (1997) *The New NHS: Modern, Dependable*, Cm 3807, London: HMSO.

Working Party on Priority Setting (1996) *Priority Setting in the NHS: A Discussion Document*, London: Working Party on Priority Setting.

—— (1998) *Priority Setting in the NHS: Experience of Priority Setting in Six Districts. Second Report of a Working Party*, London: Working Party on Priority Setting.

Zwart, H. (1993) 'Rationing in The Netherlands: the liberal and communitarian perspective', *Health Care Analysis* 1, 1: 53–6.

5

IMPOSSIBLE PROBLEMS?

The limits to the very idea of reasoning about the management of health services[1]

Michael Loughlin

This chapter discusses critically two research projects. The first is the attempt to discover, construct or invent a subject called 'the ethics of health services management', a project which involves managers and theorists from assorted academic disciplines discussing questions about how managers ought to behave, with the aim of providing practical guidance to managers on how to make their decisions 'ethically'. This guidance may take the form of general principles, which are derived or (more usually) simply posited, and which the managers are then invited (perhaps with the aid of illustrations) to apply.[2] Alternatively, it might take the form of a discussion of the goals of management, and of how managers might achieve those goals, the assumption being that in doing so managers must be doing whatever it is that they 'ought' to do.[3] Other approaches include discussion of the 'key virtues' of managers, again with the apparent assumption that managers who display or possess these virtues will, necessarily, be 'ethical' managers.[4]

The second project is the attempt to discover ethical methods of rationing health care. This process is often described in rather more sanitised terms as 'priority setting', a title which has the advantage of making the whole procedure sound a little less grim, and a little more scientific than in fact it is. This project also attempts to

68

improve practice by helping policy-makers think about what they *should* do when deciding which services to 'prioritise'. Frequently the relative claims of different groups to a share of the service's limited resources are assessed in terms of their rights, needs or capacity to benefit, and principles or purpose-built theoretical devices (such as the economists' Quality Adjusted Life Year – QALY) are proposed as solutions to the problem of how to ration ethically. The aim is to enable the ethical policy-maker (notably, often identified with 'we', the moral community – an identification typically treated as unproblematic) to discriminate systematically and in the least offensive way possible, whether it is the elderly, those who have 'irresponsible lifestyles', those whose treatments are expensive or some other, less easily identified but nonetheless real group of persons who are singled out for inconvenience, suffering and even death.

The two projects are closely related. Each represents an attempt to discuss rationally the organisation of the health service (as opposed to addressing directly issues in the *delivery* of care by specific health care professionals) and each is inevitably evaluative in nature. Theorists, including economists and other social scientists as well as philosophers and so-called 'ethicists', discuss the behaviour of managers and policy-makers alike in order to determine not only how these people do in fact behave, but how they ought to behave. The idea is not simply to describe the thought processes which lead to decisions about how health care is to be delivered, but also to affect them. The discussion would therefore be incomplete without some statement to the effect that something 'should be' the case, or about how things could be made better – some might even go so far as to say that the whole point of analysing the way the world is is to work out ways to improve it, and thus the point of analysing health service organisation is to work out how to organise health services better.

Much of the theoretical debate concerns what it *means* for the service to be better: does it mean more 'fair' according to some specific conception of justice (the Rawlsian conception being currently the most fashionable)?[5] Or does the service's being better amount to its producing more benefits (raising obvious questions about what we mean by, and how we are to measure, benefit)?[6] Should the 'values' we use to determine practice and policy be based in individualist or communitarian philosophies,[7] or does it make sense to derive them, as some economists seem to think, from some sort of empirical survey? Even theorists who purport, however implausibly, to be engaged in 'value-neutral analysis' when discussing health care policy, invariably comment on what it is right, best or most rational to do, given the assumption of certain goals whose nature and legitimacy are taken as uncontroversial.[8] Those who dislike the word 'evaluative' can substitute the word 'practical', since for our present purposes they mean the same thing: an evaluative discourse is one that aims to affect practice via the process of argument. It seems obvious that the arguments in question should be rational ones, since it is not clear how we can expect people to take what we say seriously unless we can provide them with *good reasons* to do so, and the attempt to influence practice by presenting good reasons for one's conclusions is an attempt to construct rational arguments.

In what follows I intend to argue that debates of this sort are in an important sense misguided. While there is no essential contradiction involved in trying to offer rational arguments in support of conclusions about how people ought to behave, a contradiction does emerge if one attempts to do this in the context of health service management and policy. The argument's structure is analogous to that found in certain arguments in religious philosophy: while opponents of theism usually concede that there is no inherent contradiction in the idea of an omnipotent and wholly benevolent being, they sometimes claim it is illogical to posit the existence of such a being in the context of a flawed creation.[9] Similarly, the attempt to provide an account of the decision-making processes that form health service policy which is at once 'realistic' (taking the service as it is as its starting point) and 'pragmatic' (attempting to affect its nature via rational argument) fails, given the real nature of the context in which the decisions under discussion take place. The very idea that such an account might be possible derives from an assumption (to be spelled out in detail in what follows) which is both ideological in character and patently false. Indeed, it is only because the assumption in question is embedded firmly in the ideology dominant in our culture that it normally escapes critical attention, such that its influence and evident falsity remain unrecognised. Theorists who write in this area have to face the possibility not only that their work cannot do any positive good, but also that it may be positively harmful, in that it serves to endorse some of the central myths of contemporary society, and so by its very existence threatens to distort that which it purports to analyse.

70

Given that the likely readers of this paper include such theorists, asking them to consider this possibility may be like asking a group of evangelical faith healers to consider the idea that there is no God, and thus that miracles cannot happen; or like asking a group of international industrialists to consider the (obviously true) proposition that capitalism is immoral, and thus that global capitalism is global immorality. Even so, unless we use acceptability to a specified group of professionals as a criterion of truth, we have no *good* reasons not to take this possibility seriously. If I am right, then we have to think very carefully about how we are to discuss the problems of the health service, in order to say anything that is at once true and worth saying. This task may be far more difficult than some theorists are prepared to admit.

IN DEFENCE OF NEGATIVITY

I shall argue that each of the projects under discussion is impossible, and for the same reason. Each is generated by a specific set of social and economic conditions, and each one assumes that rational moral debate about the organisation of health services is possible given those conditions.[10] This assumption is necessary if either project is to be possible. However, I shall argue that it is also false, so neither project is possible.

This conclusion will strike many readers as negative, and some will view this as a problem for my argument (rather than viewing the argument as presenting a problem for the assumptions it criticises). There is a common tendency in any 'practical' discussion to view an analysis as having *failed* (or at least as being somehow incomplete) if it has 'failed to come up with' any positive conclusions. Readers who react in this way should think very carefully about what it means to *criticise* an argument for having negative conclusions. Do they think that a 'negative' conclusion is less likely to be true than a 'positive' one? Is it that the truth doesn't matter, that 'being positive' is all that matters?

Such a response is ideological and deeply reactionary. We all know the sort of regime which insists that all news must be good news. The view that all arguments must be 'positive' is a peculiar academic variant on this theme. It has its basis in a consumerist view of the social world which now seems to permeate our thinking on almost every issue. On this view the purpose of a piece of writing cannot be naively to state the truth, in an attempt to communicate with other rational beings who have the desire to understand their world. Rather what one says, to be worth saying at all, must be 'useful'. What is more, the conception of 'usefulness' at work here (unlike conceptions of usefulness employed in more credible forms of philosophical pragmatism) implies that what one says must be of use to some group whose role is defined in terms of the existing social order, such as the role of the policy-maker or manager. Only then can one's argument have a 'market', and only then can one be justified in stating it in the first place. Indeed, it is assumed, if one is writing about management and/or policy, that these are just the groups one's work should be *for*, so a critique of the social order which gives rise to these roles, which defines their nature and goals, 'offers nothing' to those working within that order, and so can be dismissed out of hand: not because it is wrong, but because no-one wants to 'buy' its conclusions.

Thus it becomes impossible to criticise the prevailing social and economic order, or to identify *it* as the main obstacle in the way of human beings searching for humane solutions to the problems they encounter. (It becomes, effectively, impossible to get people to think 'beyond their roles'; a point I return to later.) All arguments are set the task of proving how, given the established order, real and meaningful solutions to pressing moral problems can be found. The statement 'the system works' acquires by default the status of a logical truth, since what it is for any proposed solution to 'work' has to be explained with reference to the system as it is: either an argument does, or does not, make the attempt to show that morally adequate solutions can be found by working within the limits on human action defined by the system as it is. If it does not then it can *for that very reason* be dismissed as not 'practical'. (Radical criticisms of the dominant system and its ideology are often rejected, it is claimed, *because* they are not practical. The truth is quite the reverse: they are not considered practical *because* they are incompatible with that system and its ideology. The ideological framework rules out consideration of any alternative to itself, and so appears to be no more than 'common sense' to those working within it.)[11]

The same mentality is at work in much of the apparently ad hoc linguistic legislation and verbal tinkering that characterises contemporary management thinking. (A more honest, if less polite label would be 'anti-thinking', since so much of the work in this area does its best to discourage critical thought, and some of it openly eschews rationality for being 'unhelpful' to the goals of management.)[12] Management theory is a liturgy of positive thinking, imploring us to 'focus positive', to speak not of 'weaknesses' or 'failings' but of 'areas for improvement', to use words which 'empower action', and to be 'obsessed' not with the world as it is and the horrors it contains, but with our inspirational 'vision' of how it might be.[13]

The desire to be positive also explains the attractiveness of the term 'priority setting' in contrast with 'rationing'. Any rational creature with finite means sets priorities: talking in this way enables us to focus on that which is achieved, rather than dwelling on failures. Our intellectual starting point is not a highly developed complex service already providing many forms of care; instead we begin by thinking of a blank sheet, a scenario in which nothing is provided. This mental shift serves the same psychological purpose as the phrase 'today is the first day of the rest of your life'. We are invited to imagine ourselves starting as if from nothing, at the dawn of a new day, with everything still to do. Then, instead of deciding which services have to be cut, we think about which to provide. Against this benchmark any provision at all becomes an achievement. The implicit comparison with a single, rational creature deciding which goals to set itself, helps us to forget that the 'de-prioritised' services are not simply goals which we (the 'rational community') have – temporarily or permanently – decided prudently to give up, but that they represent depriving some individuals of the means of a bearable existence, and sometimes of life itself. As I shall argue, it also encourages us to *delude* ourselves about our powers: specifically, about the locus of decision-making in our own societies.

Even authors who talk a great deal of sense about this subject seem determined to be 'positive' about the topic, and so to avoid expressions such as 'rationing'. Despite using the word in the title of his paper, Klein (1993: 96) suggests that the word 'rationing' is too 'emotional'.[14] The prevailing idea, which comes across most strongly in the works of authors such as Williams (1995), is that if we get upset about the fact that people have to suffer and die, this somehow must cloud our judgement. It is somehow bad taste to make a fuss about such things which are, after all, 'necessary'. If we despair of finding an adequate solution this only indicates our lack of moral and/or intellectual stamina (rather than, for instance, clear-sightedness and intellectual honesty). There just *has to* be a solution: that is 'pure common sense'.

There is very little in this world that is *absolutely* necessary: most of the things we call 'necessary' are only necessary given certain conditions. It is both astonishing and revealing that many theorists writing about health seem to be of the opinion that it is not their business to examine critically the conditions which *necessitate* the problems they discuss. Whether they realise it or not, such theorists assume the role of apologists for and servants to the status quo. Their 'practical' work involves helping the whole machine tick over effectively, or, failing that, explaining that the reason why it does not tick over right now is because no-one has yet thought of the theory which will fix it: there is simply no question that the machine may have a structural fault, that it is beyond fixing – however many broken bodies it churns out.

My arguments hope to be 'useful' only in the very broad sense in which any philosophical argument may claim to be useful. Good philosophy analyses the fundamental assumptions which underlie a discourse, and philosophy can take any serious human discourse as the object of its study: be it religious discourse, scientific discourse or the language of specific practical moral arguments. The assumptions studied are often treated as too obvious to be worthy of serious critical attention by those engaged in the discourse, and yet it is possible to examine them for coherence and plausibility, and indeed to discover that they do not stand up well to scrutiny: they may turn out to be highly controversial or even palpably false.

This way of thinking will be attractive to any rational being with the desire to understand his or her own situation, and the wider context of which it is a part. It enables us to think not only within the confines of the roles and positions we happen to occupy, but also to treat those roles and the structure in which they have their being as the object of our study. By thinking of our condition from the 'outside' in this way we may find that we are able to gain a greater insight into the real nature of our problems and perhaps even to discover that their *solution* also lies beyond the limits of the roles we presently perform. This may be an uncomfortable realisation. It may be a huge task to work out how one responds to such a realisation. Nonetheless, the activity which gives rise to it is a prerequisite for reflective human thought, and one cannot develop a meaningful response to one's own condition until one has taken the trouble to reflect seriously on what, precisely, one's condition *is*.

In the following section I will describe the context in which the problems for managing health services ethically come about. The description will be very brief: its function is only to bring out certain *key* features relevant to the discussion to follow. I will then consider certain proposed solutions to these problems, showing them to be spurious by arguing that the methods they use to 'solve' problems are in fact loaded, such that any answer one cares to give can be deemed correct. (Thus they function not as solutions to real problems but as a *rationale* for any specific answer one might want to defend.) I shall go on to take each of the projects in turn – the attempt to construct an 'ethic for managers' and the attempt to construct an 'ethic for rationing' – showing each one to be guilty of the same error, and turning my attention finally to the nature of that error and its pervasiveness in contemporary political conversation.

PROBLEM AND CONTEXT

There is an intimate link between the very existence and character of the modern health service manager and the existence and character of the rationing debate. The intellectual environment of each is shaped and limited by certain assumptions of market economics, the key one being the central economic assumption of 'scarcity' (Williams 1995: 221). (This is why economists are so obviously at home in discussing both management and rationing.) It is in the face of scarcity that managers are charged to 'lead, develop, control and evaluate' the work of carers (Wall 1989: 2) in order to facilitate an *efficient* use of health service resources. Thus managers often view themselves as 'guardians' of the public interest (Institute of Health Services Management [IHSM] 1993: 24), ensuring that no part of the service wastes vital resources which could be better employed elsewhere. *Because* health resources are scarce, it would be *wrong* to waste them. An inefficient use of resources in one area leads *inevitably* to others being deprived of services they need: hence the moral imperative to find the most efficient (meaning 'cost-effective') organisation of services (Williams 1992) and, as a consequence, the need for a group of persons whose job it is to introduce these ideas into the day-to-day running of the health service.

Any attempt to reason seriously about what 'efficiency' means in this context will encounter a variety of deep conceptual problems. To do the job properly it would be necessary to develop a theory that allowed us to measure the value of the many diverse benefits of different health care activities, in sufficiently precise terms to be able to feed them into a cost-benefit calculation. Apart from the apparently insurmountable epistemological problems in knowing how specific interventions affect the lives of diverse patients, and the total absence of any adequate theory of value or account of the nature of benefit that could make quantification meaningful, the task seems to be rendered logically impossible since all too often we are dealing with *incommensurable* values. Even management theorists occasionally admit this: 'How can anyone choose between more staff for the special care baby unit and additional domicilary care for the elderly mentally confused; they have nothing in common but are equally deserving' (Wall 1989: 43).

In addition to the problems in identifying and measuring benefits, there are deep problems involved in identifying and measuring costs, especially once we accept that not all costs are financial. How does one measure the psychological and material damage suffered by persons (and their families) deprived of employment as a result of 'labour saving' management innovations? (Loughlin 1994: 311). What value (or rather disvalue) ought we to place upon the stress and sense of 'alienation' suffered by carers forced to work to 'productivity' targets that seem to them not only irrelevant to the nature of their work, but blind to its true value? (Darbyshire 1993). The very attempt to put a figure on such costs would seem to falsify their nature: like so many features of human life, to treat them as something which one can quantify is to fail to understand them.

One standard theoretical response to such difficulties (with a long pedigree in economic theory) is to ignore them. Features of the context which cannot be quantified can, it is assumed, be left out of the calculation, but a meaningful calculation can still be performed. Here theory seems to be dictating the nature of reality in a disturbing sense, since we effectively treat as unreal any features of the world which cannot be incorporated into our cost-benefit analysis. It makes little sense to say that I have a 'good' explanation of a series of events because I ignore all the evidence which my explanation cannot account for; just so, it seems entirely ad hoc to claim that we can have an adequate theory of decision-making based on a device for measuring value, because we systematically ignore all the features of the world to which our device is insensitive. The only possible justification for giving such a response is the assumption that there *must* be some adequate way of making these decisions and, given the nature of social reality, appeal to such devices represents the *only* practical way of doing this. The 'best answer available to us' must, it is assumed, be 'adequate' and must effectively be treated as the 'right' answer, since the idea that neither the right, nor even the adequate, answers are available to us must be ruled out in advance. (I have already commented upon the attitudes which underlie this sort of response. I will bring out the picture of social reality which gives rise to these attitudes in more detail in the following sections.)

The similarities between this discussion and the rationing debate are obvious. The latter represents an attempt to discover how practice 'ought to be conducted, in the face of scarcity, if our objective is to maximise the benefits of health care' (Williams 1995: 221).

The main difference between the two projects seems to be the level at which arguments are usually pitched, and the assumptions which are consequently made by contributors to the debate about its audience. The 'ethics of management' typically concerns questions about the day-to-day running of services, and it is assumed that the primary 'target audience' for texts and articles written is made up of managers. Thus some contributors to the debate seem to think that it is a sign of an argument's success that it 'draws the crowds in health management' (Wall 1994). If we are thinking of success in commercial terms then this may be correct, although we usually think of an argument's success or failure in terms of its validity and the truth of its premises and conclusions. (As I argued above, the tendency to confuse the two is part of a rather disturbing trend.)

In contrast there is a *tendency* for arguments about rationing to be directed at 'policy-makers' and, significantly, they are often phrased in the first person plural. (The implications of identifying policy-makers with a group characterised by the term 'we' will be discussed in the final section of this chapter.) Thus, discussions tend to address the *overall* distribution of resources in an economy, although, as Klein (1993: 96) points out, even this is not an essential or defining characteristic of the debate, since any resource allocation decision, at any level, may legitimately be viewed as an instance of 'priority setting'. There seems, then, to be no definitive or logically tight distinction between the two projects here analysed. Rather, each one is an aspect of the broader debate about how to organise health services ethically, in the face of social circumstances which make the provision of a comprehensive service economically impossible.

Clearly, then, the same conceptual problems arise for each project. Each must attempt to evaluate the relative merits of alternative options whose practical effects are only partially known, and whose relative values appear to resist quantification and are often incommensurable. This problem is only exacerbated if we insist that there are other essential requirements of an ethical organisation, in addition to efficiency. It may well be that there is more to the rationing debate than the question of how to maximise benefits, since even the maximally beneficial distribution (if one had some way of determining what this might be) could be objected to on the grounds that it was unjust. (Chadwick 1993: 85) This generates further potentially intractable problems. We then have to decide not only who can benefit most from some specific type of treatment (taking all possible alternative benefits and costs into account), but also who has the most 'right' to it, where, it seems, there is more to having the right to a given benefit than having the capacity to be benefited or harmed by the result of the decision; more, even, than being the person who would benefit more from the treatment in question than anybody else. However, if these problems exist then they equally affect the ethics of health management, and hence they do not serve to *distinguish* the rationing debate from the debate about management ethics.[15] The *object* of each project is the same: to find the best way (whatever counts as 'best') of depriving some people of services they need because scarcity makes it impossible to meet every need. The contributors to each debate prefer, for reasons already gone into, to focus on 'how to achieve the most given our limitations' rather than 'how to sacrifice the least (and with the least injustice) *because of* those limitations', but the reality is the same from whichever perspective we choose to view it. Take away the background of scarcity and you would have no debate: this context is as fundamental to our topic as is the material world to physics.

As economists never tire of pointing out, one solution not available is to deny the existence of scarcity, or to complain that if we only spent more money on health the problem would go away. This is, unfortunately, impossible to deny, although more attention should be given to the question of precisely *why* this is the case. It seems essential to the nature of contemporary society that it generates more sickness than it can cure. Short of a radical change in the nature of society, which would *abolish* the problem and make all proposed solutions superfluous, there will always be some people with needs that could, in principle, be met, but which will not be met in practice because there are many more legitimate claims on the service than it can satisfy.

This characterisation of the problem suggests one, rather swift, solution, which for convenience I shall refer to as 'the easy solution'. One could argue that, since 'ought' implies 'can', and since a legitimate claim is one that ought to be met, not all of the claims on the service can really be legitimate, since they cannot all be met. Those claims which the service cannot meet are not, therefore, legitimate claims.

To borrow a phrase from Bertrand Russell, this solution has all the advantages of theft over honest toil. How can a claim, which would otherwise be judged legitimate, become illegitimate as a result of factors which have nothing to do with the needs of the (potential) patient? Either those needs provide the basis for a legitimate claim, or they do not. If they do not then there is no legitimate claim on the service, even if the resources *are* available. If they do (and the whole rationing debate is predicated on the reality that there are many such claims which cannot be met) then how can their legitimacy be wiped away by extraneous economic factors? If my lifestyle is such that I cannot pay all my debts, does it follow that they cannot really be my debts after all? Might we not conclude that I should change my lifestyle? Verbal games cannot disguise the fact that real people, with real needs, are being made to suffer, and if this turns out to be an inevitable consequence of the nature of the society in which they live, then why not conclude that there is something fundamentally wrong with that society?

The problem with a society, in contrast to at least some human individuals (the ones, significantly, that we view as possessing rational self-control) is that it is not easy to get it to 'change its ways': the very idea that a complex society can simply decide, on the basis of a rational argument, to make fundamental changes to its internal organisation is based on an unrealistic view of the processes of social change. This point is often recognised but its implications for the nature of rational debate *about* society, and the limitations it places on such debate, often go unrecognised. The difficulties in using reason to affect change in the structure of society give rise to difficulties for the project of rationally affecting change in any substantial *sector* of the whole structure. To abstract that sector from the structure which gives it its being, to treat it in isolation, ignores the important relationships it has with the rest of the structure, and so one is able to have a 'pragmatic' discussion, presenting proposals for practical change, at the expense of realism. (Therefore one's pragmatism is *deluded*.) The more realistic one becomes, the more one recognises the relationships with wider features of the whole which determine the nature of the sector under discussion, the more implausible it becomes to assume that one can change the nature of this reality by proving that it could, in so many ways, be much better. However impeccable the proof, there is no relationship between the impeccability of an argument and its causal efficacy in facilitating social change.

We find this tension between pragmatism and realism hard to accept; the vast majority of academic arguments ignore it altogether. This may be partially due to frustration: we find it hard to reconcile the idea that some feature of our own society could and should be better with the assertion that we are in no position to make it any better. However, the correct way to deal with frustration cannot be to deny the nature of the reality which frustrates one's hopes or ideals. It is interesting that we do not have any such problem when thinking about societies other than our own. We are happy to entertain the idea that many societies in history – doubtless ones 'less developed' than ours – may have been afflicted by problems which they simply could not solve, because the conditions were not right for an adequate solution to be found and implemented. There is a Hegelian tendency to see one's own society as the end-product of the whole process of evolution, and so to assume either that it cannot get any better, or that, if it can, the means to *make* it better are readily available to its inhabitants, if they'll just give it some thought.

I return to this assumption, and the reasons why we are inclined to make it, in the final section. For the moment I want to return to the easy solution. It is obvious that it will not do, but it is worth thinking for a moment about why it will not do. It provides us with no systematic way of making the relevant decisions about who must suffer and/or die. It simply tells us that whichever decisions we make, we can retrospectively judge them to have been right, since those we chose to deprive of care had no legitimate claim in the first place, in virtue of the very fact that they were not selected. It is the sort of argument which old-fashioned philosophy books would call an 'apology', only it is not an apology for any specific position or decision, but rather for any position on this issue which those making the decisions might care to take up. If they decide to discriminate against the elderly then they can argue that they were right to do so. If they decide to discriminate against the young then again they are right. The argument does not so much guide as rubber-stamp decisions. It is absurd to describe any argument as providing a 'defence' of a particular position or decision if it equally counts as a defence of the contrary position or decision. An argument which is compatible with both X and −X does not *establish* either. An argument which justifies anything you like justifies nothing in particular.

In contrast, then, a good argument would be one which determines a particular decision by giving it an adequate theoretical basis. That is to say, one should be able to deduce *determinate answers* to questions about how one ought to allocate health resources; ones that could be directly applied to practice. One should be able to say that certain decisions are (or would be) the right ones, and others would be wrong, and to provide a justification for that claim in terms of the theory of ethical decision-making offered. Otherwise, what precisely is the theoretical debate *about*? If the work of theorists does not provide a clear method for criticising some decisions, and for advocating others, then it does not really affect practice; except by creating the *appearance* that decisions made have a grounding in theory. (That is not to say that theorists cannot address foundational questions. However, there is no sense in laying foundations if one never intends to build on them. As a matter of logic, foundations must be foundations *for* whatever is to be founded upon them. If no practical implications can be derived from a foundational argument about ethics, then the argument is flawed.)[16]

Bearing this in mind, it is worth looking at a couple of arguments which may be attractive to some practitioners precisely because they create the *appearance* that there is an adequate theoretical basis for decisions in practice. They invite people to go through a process of deliberation before making decisions, but the process does not determine any particular decision, nor does it in fact determine any specific attitude towards life in general which could then affect decisions. Having contemplated the theoretical arguments, decision-makers are still obliged to choose on the basis of their own subjective reactions, just as they would have done had they never encountered the theory. What it offers them is a bogus sense of reassurance that they have some ethical 'grounding' which they didn't have before. This can then be used as a weapon in argument whenever their decisions are questioned. So these arguments are essentially similar to the easy solution, but because they are expressed in more complex terms their logical status is not as readily apparent. The Russellian retort does not acknowledge that some types of theft can be hard work. If the easy solution is analogous to snatching a wallet and running at top speed, the solutions I want to consider now are akin to corporate fraud

PROPOSED SOLUTIONS

The first solution I want to look at concerns specifically the project of constructing an 'ethic for health services management', and can be found in Andrew Wall's book *Ethics and the Health Services Manager* (1989). This solution is interesting because Wall apparently accepts the points I have been making about the incommensurability of values and the limits on rational thought in the context of the modern health service. He states: 'Obviously, choosing ways to spend [health] resources is not a rational process. It is largely influenced by assumptions and powerful groups, all as potent as they are non-rational' (Wall 1989: 101).

Wall has since explicitly rejected the idea that rationality has anything to do with management (Wall 1994). It would surely follow from this that no statement about how managers 'ought' to conduct themselves could be capable of justification since, as I argued above, the attempt to give good reasons for one's conclusions is the attempt to construct rational arguments. If the latter is impossible in the context of health service management, then so is the former. In which case, it follows that no-one can have any reason to take seriously anything Wall or anyone else has to say on the subject of what managers 'ought to do'. The discipline 'the ethics of health services management' is therefore impossible.

Undeterred, Wall purports to offer 'practical guidance' to managers about how to conduct themselves 'ethically', by taking certain 'everyday dilemmas' and examining them 'within a simple ethical framework' (Wall 1989, preface). He posits several 'principles' asserting that patients have certain 'rights' including:

'that their individuality be respected'; 'that those looking after them should exert their best skills on the patient's behalf' and 'that no unreasonable harm should come to them' (Wall 1989: 11).

At several points, Wall accepts that such statements do not have a very clear and direct application to practice. For instance, he admits that 'the definition of what is "reasonable"' is 'crucial', but instead of going on to provide the crucial definition he gives an instance of expenditure which, in his view, is not reasonable (*ibid.*: 15).

Naturally, Wall refuses to give a philosophical justification for his 'principles', stating that 'matters of moral philosophy' are not his concern (*ibid.*: 2). The attempt to discuss ethics without getting involved in questions of moral philosophy is the intellectual equivalent of discussing how to build and maintain nuclear power stations, without getting bogged down in abstract discussion of theoretical physics. What exactly is accomplished? Does one have an 'ethical grounding' for one's decisions simply on the basis of having read a book with the word 'ethics' in the title? Little consideration, if any, seems to be given to the question of what it might mean to speak of an 'ethic for managers', and what conditions there are on the adequacy of any such 'ethic'. Is it meaningful to purport to 'guide' people when one accepts that no arguments can be offered to explain why anyone should follow one's 'guidance'? Is there a difference between 'ethical guidance' and 'a set of unsupported (and unsupportable) assertions'? Of course, Wall does not need to offer any defence of his 'principles' since they are phrased in such general terms that no-one in their right mind could disagree with them. (How many people think that unreasonable harm *should* befall patients, or that those looking after them *should not* use their 'best skills' in doing so?) Wall avoids giving detailed explanations of how these principles apply to practice, expecting instead that his readers will use their judgement when applying them. In other words, the gap between the principles and practice is to be bridged by the subjective decisions of particular managers, and two managers, supposedly using the same principles, could come to different decisions.

By now the similarities with the easy solution should be apparent. Anyone can issue a series of prescriptions, or assert the existence of certain 'ethical principles' without argument. Such assertions could only have any merit if they were part of a *theoretically adequate approach* to solving moral problems. An adequate approach must either give a determinate answer to a specific question, or it must provide a *method* which could generate some determinate answer in some specific situation. If my theory is so vague that it can be used to justify anything then it adds nothing to the debate, except the *feeling* that problems have been solved when clearly they haven't. Wall offers managers the chance to come to any decision they like and to *say* that it is justified in terms of ethical principles, should they feel the need to do so. The same feature which accounts for the work's popularity also guarantees its theoretical inadequacy.

The same can be said of the second solution I want to consider. The QALY is proposed as an ethical solution to the problems of rationing. One of its most prominent defenders, Alan Williams, explains the idea as follows:

> Commonsense tells us that in the face of scarcity we should use our limited resources in such a way that they do as much good as possible. In health care, 'doing good' means improving people's life expectancy and the quality of their lives. . . . The essence of the QALY concept is that effects on life expectancy and effects on quality of life are brought together in a single measure.
>
> (Williams 1995: 222)

Unlike Wall, Williams eschews neither rationality nor objectivity. The claim that 'we should . . . do as much good as possible' sounds like one of Wall's principles, but Williams attempts to provide a more precise definition of what 'doing good' in this context means. The idea of a 'QALY' is initially exciting because it offers the possibility of an objective measurement to determine what counts as 'the best thing' one could do in any given set of circumstances. In rationing, there will always be consequences which are 'unfortunate for someone or other' (*ibid.*), but at least it becomes possible to make the best of a bad lot, once we know what this *means*: the 'best' outcome being the outcome that brings about the most QALYs.

The problems arise when we attempt to give some *content* to the concept of the QALY. Williams assumes that this can be done 'empirically': 'the empirical work involved in making the concept operational is concerned with eliciting the values that people attach to different health states . . . ' (*ibid.*). In other words, to find out what is really most valuable, we ask people to tell us what, as a matter of fact, they value. This simply assumes a subjectivist theory of value: it takes it as read that people cannot be wrong about the values they attach to things. Williams may not be troubled by the fact that this is a huge assumption, totally without support in his work. He should perhaps be more troubled by the fact that, understood properly, it would render the whole project in which he is engaged meaningless. First, if all value judgements are subjective, then there is no sense to asking what anyone 'ought' to do about anything, since we can have no basis for a rational debate about any practical question. If people share our subjective reactions then there is no need for a debate, and if they don't then we can only hope to sway them, by non-rational persuasion, round to our way of thinking. So the attempt to discuss how the health service ought to be organised using rational, academic arguments is misguided, unless subjectivism about values is a false theory. (I defend these points in more detail in Loughlin 1994.)

Second, it makes no sense to ask what 'we' value most, when 'we' refers to a group whose members disagree about values, both with one another, and each member with him or herself, over time (since people change their minds about what they value). Each person can say 'what is valuable for me, now' (the fact that they might not be sure, and might have to give it a great deal of thought, should suggest that there is *something* wrong with the subjectivist assumption), but there is no intellectually defensible way to move from the activity of soliciting and recording such judgements to a view about what is 'really' valuable, or 'most' valuable.

The similarities between the QALY approach and the easy solution start to emerge when we consider Williams' response to such problems (or rather his dismissal of them, since he does not think that they are really problems for the QALY at all). He is fully aware that any policy-maker using the QALY device to make rationing decisions would have to make decisions about whose values to count (since obviously it would not be possible to question every person affected by a policy), and how to move 'from individual values to group values'. He also acknowledges that there are distinct questions which the QALY cannot answer about how benefits are distributed, once we have discovered the 'amount' of benefits which accrue from specific health service activities (Williams 1995: 224).

Williams seems quite content to accept that there can be no determinate answer to such questions. As a health economist, it is 'not for him to say' (*ibid.*) how the device is employed in practice, and he treats the flexibility of the QALY when it comes to answering such questions (meaning, its ability to leave any answer open when it comes to such questions) as one of its virtues: 'the QALY is extremely accommodating in this respect. In principle it can accept any body's views about what is important in health-related quality of life, and any body's views about the trade-off between length and quality of life' (*ibid.*). On the move 'from individual to group values' he says: 'there is nothing in the QALY approach which requires aggregation to be accomplished in any particular way' (*ibid.*).

He then describes distinct ways of arriving at the 'collective' view, following the soliciting of individual views, making it clear that a variety of different and incompatible 'collective' views could purport to be 'based on' the individual views expressed. Similarly, on the issue of the distribution of benefits: 'there is nothing in the QALY approach which requires QALYs to be used only in a maximising context' (*ibid.*). One might determine the 'collective' view in a way that did not involve 'QALY maximisation' as the 'collective prioritising rule'.

The theoretical adequacy of the QALY in determining the 'best' allocation of resources must surely be questioned, once we realise that it is compatible with many distinct, and mutually incompatible, methods for arriving at practical decisions. The objectivity of this approach is illusory, since there is no determinate answer to the question of how we organise the information acquired empirically; nor can there be any answer to the question of whether the views solicited in any empirical survey represent the 'right' answers, for the whole approach implicitly accepts that there are no right answers.

This same flexibility makes it useful to policy-makers, since given the right method of aggregation a wide variety of policies could be given 'justification' with reference to the QALY. The device is also very 'accommodating' to those who want to make 'priority setting' seem more rational, since in addition to its bogus 'objectivity' it successfully disguises the incommensurability of many of the values involved in decisions about the allocation of health resources. By insisting that people rank options, we assume that a ranking is intelligible: effectively, we make it a matter of necessity that all values must be commensurable. Thus, the problem of incommensurability is systematically ignored, and it is assumed that it must always be in principle possible to make a rational choice between two options. (A point which Wall rightly treated as obviously false.) Williams' 'empirical' methods make decisions which can only be arbitrary appear non-arbitrary, by disguising the arbitrary origins of the so-called 'judgements' on which they are based.

These points aside, the QALY device assumes implicitly the legitimacy of the economic structure which determines scarcity, by taking as read every feature of social reality other than the health service. There are many determinants of the length and quality of life, but Williams only considers the effects of *medical* interventions. He states that 'in a resource-constrained system "cost" means "sacrifice"' (Williams 1995: 223), arguing that benefits given to one patient necessarily lead to benefits being forgone by others. As I have pointed out, something is only necessary *given* certain conditions, and Williams chooses to examine no other features of the social world than medical services. This effectively assumes that every other feature of the economy is 'beyond question', or that it is not 'our' business to question it, because 'we' are concerned with health care policy. But there is no reason for human beings to bind themselves to thinking in categories arbitrarily dictated by the political structure as it is, as if thinking about health care means imagining oneself to be the 'minister responsible for health care', and imagining what one should do with one's limited budget (assuming that the possibility of persuading the chancellor to give health a bit more is out of the question).

It is not clear that having an intelligent view about health means thinking of the health service in isolation from the rest of social reality, imagining 'other things are equal'. The ascription of causal efficacy to one feature of social reality is neither a naive nor a value neutral activity. To say that spending in one area of the health service leads necessarily to shortages in another area is not to make a purely 'empirical' observation. Rather, Williams performs a thought-experiment in which he assumes that every other feature of the world is the same, *except* that the benefits which in fact went to one group of patients might instead have been allocated to a different group. Noting that in that case things would have been better for the second group and worse for the first, he concludes that the benefits enjoyed by the first group *necessitated* the sacrifices made by the second. But one might equally argue that increased salaries for the leaders of industry 'necessitated' the sacrifices made by the second group. For one can imagine a situation in which the first group enjoyed the same benefits, and in which no sacrifices were made by the second group either, since the salaries of the rich were cut dramatically and the money saved was spent on the second group. It all depends on which counter-factual one chooses to think about, and that in turn depends on one's political position. Williams' position, like that of any naive participant in the 'rationing' debate, is inherently reactionary.

Williams might perhaps respond to this by claiming that he is only being realistic, since the health service *is* a 'resource-constrained system'. This would be to miss the point. Which counter-factual one chooses to think about does *not* depend on how 'realistic' one is: as a matter of logic, to think about a counter-factual situation is to think about a situation which is not real. Unwillingness to think about radical changes in the organisation of social reality when trying to determine what is right or best, reflects not realism but the unwillingness to admit any major differences between the way the world is and how it ought to be. It suggests the disposition to believe that the world is just about right as it is, that the social background to health service policy is morally uncontroversial.

Thus I am not complaining that the world is not 'perfect', in which case Williams would answer that we just have to make the best of it. My claim is that we have no way of determining what 'making the best of it' means. The assumption that there must be a defensible, determinate answer to questions about who should be allowed to suffer and die is false. To take a typical sort of discussion from the rationing debate, not only is it not obvious that we can find an acceptable rational answer to the question: 'should the elderly (who have worked all their lives, contributed to the system, etc.) be sacrificed, for the sake of the very young (who have all their lives ahead of them, who are innocent, etc.)?' The very idea that we *can* do so is offensive nonsense, and the attempt to construct devices or principles which enable people to make such decisions 'ethically' is an attempt to make nonsense of ethics. Why should the categories mentioned be capable of being fed into any calculation or decision-making procedure, however sophisticated, which weighs their relative moral merit? Should society ever evolve beyond its present state of semi-barbarism, such questions will not be answered but rather abolished. (I recognise that this would involve not only social development, but also accompanying advances in understanding.) Theory may be able to help this process in some small way, but theorists who purport to be able to solve our present problems only add to the moral and intellectual chaos of the modern world, by reassuring us that if we think about it in the right way, the unacceptable becomes acceptable. Viewed in the right light, phrased in the right language, the brutality and injustice inherent in any rationing procedure can, it seems, become rational and just.

THE MYTHOLOGY OF LIBERALISM

There is no such thing as an innocent question. All questions contain assumptions, and some of those assumptions might be false. For instance 'Have you stopped beating your wife yet?' assumes that the person addressed at one time engaged in wife-beating. If this assumption is false then the question has no determinate answer. It should not be answered, for it is misleading. Merely by asking it we risk distorting reality.

What assumptions are involved in the question: 'How should we manage/organise health services?' Are those assumptions false or misleading? Should we attempt to answer the question?

I have already given some arguments to the effect that we should not attempt to answer it, and that we should perhaps ask a different question: 'What are the conditions which make an adequate solution to the organisation of health services impossible?'

The first and second questions make incompatible assumptions. To embark on the project of answering one is to reject the other. Unlike Williams, who is 'constantly amazed' by objections to his theories, I expect resistance to what I am saying here. The desire to stay with the first, and reject the second question, is very strong. Our reluctance to embrace the idea that an answer to the first question is impossible, reveals deep commitments to ways of conceiving of ourselves and our relationship with the world around us. In this section I hope to bring out the nature and origin of these commitments. It is our fundamental conviction that we are members of a 'rational community' which gives sense to the project of attempting to organise health services ethically, both on the day-to-day level of management decisions, and in terms of the broader aspects of the debate about policy with respect to rationing. It is because we make this assumption that the problems of incommensurability do not seem totally destructive to the project. Surely, we think, the social world is *our* world. *We* create it, so it *cannot* give rise to problems that we cannot possibly solve. There must be some answer to the problem of incommensurable values, and so we are willing to treat solutions such as the QALY, and even the resort to a lottery system,[17] with some sympathy.

It does seem reasonable to assume that the social world (in contrast to the physical world) is created by the interactions of human beings. It does not follow that 'we' control that which we create. For we do not create it deliberately, with forethought. Its nature is not the product of rational planning. As one author points out (echoing Wall's points about the obvious lack of rational planning in resource allocation) very few of the services available to us are allocated on the basis of rational deliberation of any kind, and certainly health service policy is not determined by rational processes:

> What is available is, in some combination, a product of commercial investment, political pressure . . . individual preference, power struggles between different disciplines, collective bias and so on. In other words, what is available is governed by the very messy real world cultural and historical context, and not by planning according to rational principle.
>
> (Seedhouse 1995b)

This affects the credibility not only of attempts to affect social policy via rational arguments, but also of attempts to influence the practice of specific professional groups, and thus the project of professional ethics, including management ethics. To take the second of these first, I am not concerned here with the precise definition of a 'profession', nor, therefore, with questions about whether or not management counts as a 'profession'. My concern is simply with the project of constructing an ethic for a group of people who are identified in terms of a specific social role they perform, that is, the job they do.

The idea is to give advice to members of the group on how to develop adequate moral responses to problems peculiar to it. Since the identity of the group is defined in terms of the social role its members collectively perform, the conclusions of the arguments (certain moral assertions or prescriptions) are taken to be valid for specific persons, on the assumption that they occupy particular social roles. The legitimacy of the social roles in question is beyond the scope of the project, and must be assumed. (It is not the case that authors are 'neutral' about the moral status of the roles they discuss. The attempt to discuss how members of a profession can behave 'ethically' assumes that there are no compelling moral objections to the profession itself. It is no accident that there are no books called *Professional Ethics for Torturers*.)

There is nothing in principle wrong with this sort of enquiry, so long as it allows that one possible conclusion will be that there are *no* adequate solutions to the problems being considered, because the nature and circumstances of the social roles in question leave too little scope for individuals to reason in the way serious moral thinking requires. I suspect, however, that a theorist (or 'ethicist') who comes up with that sort of answer too often will be deemed to have *failed*: to succeed in this area is to provide principles or 'decision-making tools' that are 'practical', which means that they work within the context given, rather than complaining that the scope for rational thought is too limited by that context for its application to be meaningful. Implicit is the assumption that the context does not create problems that resist rational solution. But there is no reason why this should not be so. There is no reason why 'What is the right (or best) thing for a person in role X to do in circumstances ABC?' will necessarily have a determinate answer. Indeed, given the largely arbitrary, non-rational processes which shape professional roles, it is highly unlikely that this will always, or even very often, be the case. As we have seen, this is not, and cannot very often be the case for health services management. Thus, the context which gives rise to the role also renders impossible rational solution to the ethical problems it encounters.

The whole idea of solving moral problems by constructing 'professional ethics' strikes me as odd in any case, and it seems particularly strange that philosophers have been involved in such projects. A key virtue of philosophy is its ability to enable individuals to think beyond their roles (as explained above). Professional ethics usually take the form of quasi-legal codes for members of specific professional groups, the implication being that when such codes are developed and followed people will be behaving 'rationally' and 'ethically'. This idea would only make sense if the rational significance of the relevant professional roles were clear, if instead of being shaped by a variety of possibly conflicting historical forces, these roles were created for a clearly understood moral purpose, having a place within some rational social design. Otherwise, the codes are far more likely to function as a *substitute* for critical, rational thinking.

A properly *philosophical* response to the problems of practice in an irrational context could do no more (and no less) than give sense to individuals' feelings of frustration; that is, to articulate the sense that no matter what you do there is no satisfactory answer, and to confirm that far from being 'negative' and 'unhelpful' such feelings represent the most rational, objective and human response: indeed, they are a prerequisite for understanding the truth about one's predicament and finding ways to cope with it. In this way philosophy can offer support to individuals placed in impossible situations by enabling them to understand the causes of their difficulties. It may well be that if I cannot find the right answer, or if none of the options available seem acceptable, this is not because I am being unreasonable, but because my *world* is unreasonable, and I am sufficiently sane to have noticed. Such a realisation is the very beginning of critical thought. Life often seems senseless because it often *is* senseless: when the conditions of life are determined largely by irrational processes it is no surprise that rational life feels so much of the time like an on-going struggle against stupidity. This is what it is.

The idea that we can change the social context of specific decisions by constructing rational arguments, (thus making life *less* irrational) has been seen to be misguided. Many theorists write with the implicit assumption that their audience is made up of (or at least includes) 'policy-makers'. This may be more an aspiration than an assumption. Thus the philosopher Dan Brock describes his fellow theorists as 'academics just hoping that an occasional policymaker might read their scholarly journal articles' (Brock 1993: 409).

For the most part, such a hope seems somewhat unrealistic. Governments make decisions in terms of many factors, few of which have anything to do with a concern to do the 'right' thing. If they did want to know what was the right thing it is unlikely that they would base their views on the contents of academic journals.

However, there are at least some theorists (Brock is one example) who *do* get to give direct advice to governments on certain policy issues, by sitting on government committees with the power to make specific recommendations. Another philosopher, Michael Lockwood, suggests that in such cases it is 'gratifying' to think that 'philosophy might impinge on the real world', in that 'Parliamentary legislation' might 'be guided by philosophical considerations' (Lockwood 1985: 55). Lockwood assumes that the presence of a *philosopher* on a government committee means that *philosophy* is influencing policy. This assumption can be flawed on two counts.

First, it suggests an unrealistic and simplistic model of policy determination. It might make sense to speak of philosophy influencing policy if a Platonic philosopher king made every policy decision (Plato 1983). I think it would still be false to speak of philosophy totally determining policy, since while the king might do his best to form every policy on the basis of moral reasoning, he would inevitably be influenced by other factors and his reasoning could often be flawed. Nonetheless, philosophy would in this case be a strong influence. The correct model of policy formation, however, in no way resembles the idea of an individual following certain reasoning processes which directly determine a decision. A two-level model is still far too simplistic, but it will serve to convey my point.

Imagine an overall process whose results are determined at one level by a governing process G, which selects between an indeterminate number of other, secondary processes, A,B,C ... to bring about the final results (the results being certain decisions or policies). The methods of the secondary processes are different and often opposed to one another. The governing process has its own methods for selecting which of the secondary processes to use, to bring about its desired results. (Its methods are also often in conflict with those of many of the secondary processes: were process C, for instance, the governing process, it would never select process B for any purposes whatsoever, but process G sometimes will.) It would be misleading to claim that, on the occasion when process C is selected, the methods of that process determine, or even in any real sense influence, the overall process. For process C was only selected because in this instance the results it promised to deliver were judged, by the standards of process G, to be desirable.

Now suppose that process C is philosophy (although the following points apply if we assume it is any specific academic discipline). Does philosophy really, in any meaningful sense, influence policy if some other process determines when the views of philosophers will be called on, and which philosopher will be called? When philosophers advise those whom Lockwood calls 'the powers that be' they are *not* chosen in accordance with *philosophical* criteria, nor do such criteria influence the choice of issue on which they are requested to speak: the philosophers' remit is determined by political, not philosophical considerations. To speak, in such circumstances, of philosophy 'influencing' the political process, without giving any consideration to *why* certain philosophers are asked to speak on only certain specific issues, is to promote a wilfully naive picture of the nature of government. Can anyone seriously claim to wonder why the US government called on Dan Brock (whose political position is strongly influenced by the liberal contractualist thinking of John Rawls) to comment on specific questions in medical ethics before making certain policy decisions, but then failed to procure advice on the ethics of war from anarchist professor Robert Paul Wolff (whose academic philosophical credentials are at least as impressive as those of Brock) before coming to a decision about whether to invade Iraq?

Even ignoring the significance of the process of selection, those academics who are selected take on a political role when they find themselves in the 'policy domain' (Brock 1993: 410). This brings out the second way in which the assumption made by Lockwood is flawed. It is reminiscent of the idea that by making a poor person prime minister, we ensure that the interests of the poor are represented at the highest level (rather than, instead, making one poor person no longer poor): it completely disregards the influence of context on human thought and behaviour. Brock himself seems to accept this. Describing his experiences as 'staff philosopher' on a committee advising the US government, Brock states that his goal became not to convince others, by valid arguments, of the truth of his views on specific issues, but rather 'to persuade or even to manipulate others in order to reach a desired outcome', even when this involved 'playing a little fast and loose with the truth' (Brock 1993: 411). In other words, he ceased to function *as* a philosopher on finding himself in the new context. As Brock explains, this is inevitable since the requirements of functioning in the one context ('the policy arena') necessitate abandoning the methods appropriate to a different context ('academic debate'). He could not have retained his 'credibility' as an adviser had he insisted on sticking to his 'academic ways', by being honest about his reasons for advocating specific positions and insisting on logical consistency in the implementation of policy.

Brock devotes a chapter of his book to discussing the dilemmas this creates for philosophers who sit on government committees. He does not consider the possibility that they *should not* sit on such committees. Like so many theorists, he treats the context which creates the problems he discusses as ethically uncontroversial. Yet, clearly, the process of involving academics in government decisions conveys a certain message. My father, a retired dock worker, has never been asked to advise a government committee on ethics. This is not because Brock is generally recognised as being morally superior to a common dock worker, nor is he, as a philosopher, thought to have privileged access to the truth on moral matters. (The fact that philosophers disagree with each other so radically demonstrates this.) Philosophers, and academics generally, are valued not for their personal *opinions*, but for the *methods* they employ in approaching a problem. Brock's credentials as a philosopher are established by the high standards of arguments he employs when writing as a philosopher, not by the particular views he expresses. (I do not prove myself to be as good a philosopher as Brock by asserting my agreement with whatever views Brock expresses.) By associating the *name* of philosophy with the policy process, Brock helps to convey the impression that the policies determined are the result of impartial, objective reasoning: an impression which he admits is false. Theorists who behave in this way bestow academic credibility on the processes of government in the same way that priests once bestowed divine approval, and with as little justification. If academic debate could have any impact on the 'policy process' it would surely be via figures like Brock, but by his own account he only affects the process in so far as he abandons his 'academic ways', so *they* are not part of the process.

Discussing how 'we' could make health care policy – and indeed society generally – more 'rational' and/or 'ethical' (suggesting that 'we' could 'realistically' make this or that change, and that 'we should' do so) presupposes that the relevant social and political forces are under 'our' control. However, the collective 'we' assumed here is fictional: those who in fact influence policy are not party to the debate and will not be influenced by the sort of thinking that constitutes its essential character. The very idea that they might be derives from an ideological assumption: indeed, it is rooted in a way of conceiving of the social world that is so deep-seated and seems so natural to our pre-reflective consciousness that it deserves to be viewed as part of the *mythology* of contemporary political culture.

Many of the classic texts in liberal political philosophy describe a situation in which rational human beings, in a presocial state ('state of nature') come together to create the conditions of social life (Hobbes 1968; Locke 1967; Rousseau 1947). On the basis of rational deliberations to determine what is to their mutual advantage, they agree on rules by which each person should be governed, and they construct a state to enforce those rules. From that point onwards they no longer live in a state of nature: they are now part of 'civil society' and bound by its laws and norms.

Philosophers have held a variety of views concerning the precise role that descriptions of such scenarios play in political thinking.

Clearly they do not describe the true historical origins of human society, so it is instead often claimed that they bring out certain key logical points about our social and political obligations. It strikes me that they are more fundamental to our thinking even than that. The scenario sketched is more what historian Roger Griffin would call a 'myth' (Griffin 1991). A myth in this sense is an idea or image that motivates behaviour and determines how we think of ourselves and our relationship with the world. It is an ideal which inspires emotional commitment, for which some of its adherents might even be prepared to die. For instance, the 'mythic core' of fascist ideology concerns the idea of rebirth: persons who adopt this ideology see themselves as part of a community that has been crushed by hostile forces but is on the point of rising like the phoenix to meet its destiny (Griffin 1991). We are more comfortable thinking about the myths of alien philosophies, such as fascism, than we are thinking about the myths which underlie the dominant ideology in our own culture. (Especially since that ideology tends to frown on the mythological.)

The image of a society created by free rational agents, whose rules and structure are determined by the consent of all its members for their mutual advantage, may be seen to form the 'mythic core' of liberal democratic ideology. It is certainly an idea that many find inspiring. The state, according to this view, exists to represent the collective will of those agents. Thus it makes perfect sense to engage the state in rational debate and to assume that by doing so one is helping to determine policy: any rational agent could propose a policy and if it can be demonstrated really to be advantageous then it surely will be adopted.

Griffin thinks of myths as 'non-rational' and therefore not susceptible to rational criticism. They are not supposed to be true: they are simply ideas to inspire us. This may be so, but we surely can assess rationally the decision to construe one's relationship with one's own society in terms of a particular myth. If doing so causes us to distort the nature of social reality, then doing so is irrational. Unless we construe contemporary democracies in terms of the liberal myth, much of the debate about health service ethics and policy makes no sense. Suppose we think of the state not as the expression of rational collective choice but, as William Godwin put it, a 'brute engine' (Godwin 1976). By this Godwin meant a social mechanism whose behaviour is susceptible to analysis (like any mechanism) and is sometimes, therefore, predictable, but which does not display features of rational agency. In that case, attempting to influence its behaviour by constructing rational moral arguments makes about as much sense as King Canute's tide control strategy. Surely we can ask whether or not Godwin's image comes closer to representing the truth about our present situation than the central myth of liberalism – and, indeed, conclude that it does?

The problems this creates are not restricted to discussions about such issues as the morality of rationing – they affect the whole character of political conversation in today's liberal democracies. When thinking about political issues, we tend to *imagine* ourselves in the position of a policy-maker, we think about what it would be best to do in that position, and conclude that this is what should be done. Unlike other types of evaluative discourse (for instance, a conversation between a husband and wife about which school it would be best for them to send their children to) the conclusion that 'we should' do X has no direct practical significance, since it does not determine the behaviour of those who are in fact making the decision under discussion. We talk in this way because the mythology of liberal democratic society suggests that the decisions of the democratic state are really 'our' decisions, that we 'the public' (a collection of free, rational agents) determine policy via such a process of deliberation. But as we have seen, these ideas have no bearing whatsoever on reality. Does any serious analysis of the decisions of those in power make reference to such ideas? Of course public opinion is a factor they consider, but it is for the most part not formed by rational processes, it is easily manipulated and it is only one factor in any case.

We can of course talk about what specific persons, including leaders, 'should do', morally criticising them if they fail to act as we judge that they should. If this were all that political thinking involved then we would be logically obliged to limit our critical faculties to choosing between the options presented to us by the political parties: we could not criticise the system itself, nor could we attack features of the social structure that form the background to particular decisions; the context of the decisions would have to be simply taken as read. Some philosophical conservatives would accept this, dismissing all attempts to criticise the prevailing social order as self-deluded 'rationalism' (Oakeshott 1962).

I do not accept this position, although an explanation of my rejection of it would be beyond the scope of this paper. Indeed, it is a key goal of this paper to point beyond the scope of the discussions it considers, exposing the arbitrary nature of its parameters. A *serious* consideration of the ethics of health care cannot be *limited* to conventional 'health care ethics', since this area of life cannot be understood in isolation from the wider political scene of which it is a part. A developed position in political philosophy is an *essential* requirement for a worthwhile contribution to this area. And any *adequate* position in political philosophy will embody honest accounts of the nature of capitalism and of government itself. Although what I have said here gives some indication of my views on such matters, another key goal of the paper is to suggest that theorists should not launch into a discussion of a topic unless they can do it justice, and I cannot do these enormous questions very much justice in what remains of this article. I therefore leave them for the time being.

One thing at least is clear. If rationality is to have any role in practical debate then we have to be clear about the limits and presuppositions of our discussion. Otherwise our words will implicitly deny that those limits exist, and will form part of the pretence that we live in an idealised democracy. This pretence may legitimately be described as a 'false consciousness': we are operating with a false picture of our relationship to the world, which determines the nature of our language and neutralises its ability to solve real problems. Thus theory can influence practice in a way that is harmful, by helping to create or at least to sustain illusions.

If theorists want to influence practice *helpfully* then they should address a general audience with the aim of enabling people to question common assumptions and traditional ways of conceptualising problems. In this respect philosophy can make an important contribution. Good philosophy can help to dispel illusions by attacking ideologies which peddle false pictures of the world, and by bringing out the ideological commitments in common ways of discussing problems. Instead of constructing moral codes which oversimplify social life, philosophers should try to pass on what skills they have to individuals struggling to make sense of an increasingly complex and brutish world.

Significant social change can only come from changes in social consciousness. As Godwin observed, a reflective, critical populace is a prerequisite for meaningful social change, and anything philosophers can do to encourage critical thought is therefore a worthwhile contribution to the struggle for a more decent world. Theory may have some small role in facilitating this, but it must first become aware of its own limits. We will not make the world a more rational place by pretending it already is.

NOTES

1 Some of the arguments of this paper are rehearsed in Loughlin (1995b) and Loughlin (1996) © John Wiley and Sons Ltd. Sections are reprinted with the permission of the publisher.

2 A good illustration of this approach is Wall (1989), discussed below.

3 This goal is often taken to be 'quality', or 'organisational quality'. See, for instance, Al-Assaf and Schmele (1993).

4 This idea appears to be at work in Wall (1993) and Institute of Health Services Management (1993).

5 The influence of Rawls (1971) is so pervasive that it is harder to find examples of texts which do *not* exhibit features of the Rawlsian approach than to point to ones that do. Brock (1993) exemplifies the Rawlsian approach at its best, incorporating Rawlsian assumptions about meta-ethics and justice in social policy into an overall theory of just health care provision. Daniels (1985) and Dworkin (1994) owe a debt to Rawls. Even Williams (1995: 223) attempts a justification of his QALY approach to resource allocation in terms of the Rawlsian 'veil of ignorance'. Frequently, authors incorporate Rawlsian assumptions without an explicit statement either of the extent of the influence of Rawls, or of the highly controversial nature of his theory.

6 Even when 'benefit' is defined in terms of some other concept, such as 'health gain' Godfrey (1992), the same problems arise (Loughlin 1993). Many authors attempt to combine an approach based on some conception of benefit with one based on justice, arguing that benefits must not only be maximised but distributed 'fairly'.

7 Zwart (1993) offers a critique of what he describes as the 'rigidly communitarian' approach of Callahan (1987).

8 For an excellent illustration of this, see the opening paragraph of Williams (1995). For an exposure of the spurious nature of economists' claims about value-neutrality (specifically with reference to Williams 1992), see Seedhouse (1995a).

9 The character of Ivan in Dostoyevsky (1985: 275) puts it succinctly: 'it is not God that I do not accept, but the world that he has created'.

10 I make no distinction between the words 'moral' and 'ethical'. Some writers, usually those who have studied no philosophy, think that there is an important philosophical distinction to be drawn between the two, and that 'ethical' is somehow a much more technical word than 'moral'. This might be because they think that morals are subjective whilst the word 'ethics' refers to formal, public codes. If so then their views are rooted in the very ideological assumptions which I want to criticise.

11 The many, evidently sincere, assertions that his views are just sheer common sense made by Williams (1995) provide an excellent illustration of this phenomenon. Unable to think away certain ideological

constraints, Williams is genuinely baffled that anyone can disagree with him.

12 Wall (1994) argues that rationality can be dismissed because it is 'not to the purposes' of modern management.

13 A wonderful insight into the mind of the modern health services manager is provided by Al-Assaf and Schmele (1993), which contains a great deal of (unintentionally) highly informative semi-gibberish. The most stunning paper in the collection is Keith Curtis's 'Total quality and management philosophies', which is the source of the preceding quotations and whose evangelical quality is discussed in Loughlin (1995c).

14 Klein's realistic account is to be admired. It is revealing, and unfortunate, that he feels the need to make excuses for speaking the truth, and to attempt to find implications which are not so 'negative': as if his paper could not be deemed a success until he had found something positive to say.

15 Some management theorists recognise this. Wall (1993) considers the need to manage not only 'efficiently and effectively' but also with 'justice'.

16 As I have argued elsewhere (Loughlin 1995a) the phrase 'it works in theory but not in practice' is misleading. A moral theory that cannot be applied to the real world is, in fact, a bad theory, since it is not really *about* anything.

17 Harris (1986) is most closely associated with the idea of rationing via lottery. Calls for a lottery represent a realisation that there can be no just method of rationing, matched with the stubborn belief that there *must* be one. I know of no satisfactory *argument* to explain why losers in a lottery for care should think they have been dealt with fairly. The only argument could be based in the assumption that each person involved consents. Against this two points can be made. First, it is not clear that we can determine by consent which is the best theory of justice, or even the fairest method of allocation of any particular good or service. We would have to assume in the first instance that the consent of each person is given rationally, and this is surely the point at issue: whether or not it would be rational to give our consent to allocating essential resources in this way. Second, an argument which proceeds from the assumption of universal consent to a specific method of allocation cannot count as an argument to the effect that anyone ought to consent in the first place. The only argument I can see is that there *must* be some correct method, but since there clearly isn't one, let's opt for a lottery. The correct answer would be to admit that there is no correct method and to investigate the reasons for this. (Clearly, there is no reason why anyone should think that a lottery is a fair way to allocate anything, certainly not health care, and it is amazing that anyone can think it is a fair way to allocate vast sums of money. Obsession with lotteries is an indication of widespread intellectual and moral decay, as a few people in the UK are at last realising.)

BIBLIOGRAPHY

Al-Assaf, A. and Schmele, J. (1993) *The Textbook of Total Quality in Health Care*, Delray Beach FL: St Lucie Press.

Brock, D.W. (1993) *Life and Death: Philosophical Essays in Biomedical Ethics*, Cambridge: CUP.

Callahan, D. (1987) *Setting Limits: Medical Goals in an Ageing Society*, New York: Simon and Schuster.

Chadwick, R. (1993) 'Justice in priority setting' in *Rationing in Action*, London: BMJ Publishing Group.

Daniels, N. (1985) *Just Health Care*, Cambridge MA: CUP.

Darbyshire, P. (1993) Guest editorial: 'Preserving nurse caring in a destitute time', *Journal of Advanced Nursing* 18: 507–8.

Dostoyevsky, F. (1985) *The Brothers Karamazov*, Harmondsworth: Penguin Books.

Dworkin, R. (1994) 'Prudence or Rescue?', *Fabian Review* 106, 2: 10–14.

Godfrey, C. (1992) 'Investing in health gains: an economic approach', *HFA 2000 News* 19.

Godwin, W. (1976) *Enquiry Concerning Political Justice*, Harmondsworth: Penguin Books.

Griffin, R. (1991) *The Nature of Fascism*, London: Routledge.

Harris, J. (1986) 'The survival lottery' in Singer, P. (ed.) *Applied Ethics*, Cambridge: CUP.

Hobbes, T. (1968) *Leviathan*, Harmondsworth: Penguin Books.

Institute of Health Services Management (IHSM) (1993) *Future Health Care Options, Final Report*, London: IHSM.

Klein, R. (1993) 'Dimensions of Rationing: Who should do what?' *Rationing in Action*, London: BMJ Publishing Group.

Locke, J. (1967) *Two Treatises of Government*, Cambridge: CUP.

Lockwood, M. (1985) *Moral Dilemmas in Modern Medicine*, Oxford: OUP.

Loughlin, M. (1993) 'The strange quest for the health gain', *Health Care Analysis* 1, 2: 165–9.

—— (1994) 'The silence of philosophy', *Health Care Analysis* 2, 4: 310–16.

—— (1995a) 'Dworkin, Rawls and reality', *Health Care Analysis* 3, 1: 37–44.

—— (1995b) 'Bioethics and the mythology of liberalism', *Health Care Analysis* 3, 4: 329–36.

—— (1995c) 'Brief encounter: a dialogue between a philosopher and an NHS manager on the subject of quality', *Journal of Evaluation in Clinical Practice* 1, 2.

—— (1996) 'Rationing, barbarity and the economist's perspective', *Health Care Analysis* 4, 2: 146–56.

Oakeshott,M (1962) *Rationalism in Politics*, London: Trinity Press.

Plato (1983) *The Republic*, Harmondsworth: Penguin.

Rawls, J. (1971) *A Theory of Justice*, Boston: Harvard University Press.

Rousseau, J-J. (1947) *The Social Contract*, London: Dent and Sons.

Seedhouse, D. (1995a) 'The way around health economics' dead end', *Health Care Analysis* 3, 3: 205–20.

—— (1995b) 'Why bioethicists have nothing useful to say about health care rationing', *Journal of Medical Ethics* 21: 288–91.

Wall, A. (1989) *Ethics and the Health Services Manager*, London: King Edward's Hospital Fund for London.

—— (1993) *Values and the NHS*, London: IHSM.

—— (1994) 'Behind the wallpaper: a rejoinder', *Health Care Analysis* 2, 4:317–18.

Williams, A. (1992) 'Cost-effective analysis: is it ethical?', *Journal of Medical Ethics* 18: 7–11.

—— (1995) 'Economics, QALYs and medical ethics – a health economist's perspective', *Health Care Analysis* 3, 3: 221–6.

Zwart, H. (1993) 'Rationing in The Netherlands: the liberal and the communitarian perspective', *Health Care Analysis* 1, 1: 53–6.

6

AGE AS A CRITERION OF HEALTH CARE RATIONING

Kenneth Boyd

Rationing health care for the elderly is popularly regarded as a major problem. Among the various factors responsible for what is thought to be a need for this rationing are a steady growth in the elderly proportion of the population, the demented proportion of the elderly, medicine's ability to prolong life, and the cost of providing health care. Having become aware of the problem, however, the public seems to be uncertain what to do about it. According to a newspaper report (*Daily Telegraph* 1994), most respondents to a Gallup survey on the subject said that 'retired people' should have low priority for health treatment. When asked which type of treatment care should have priority, most replied 'care offered by GPs for everyday illnesses and diseases'. The newspaper illustrated this with a photograph of a crowded GP's waiting room in which no-one, apart from the receptionist, appeared to be under 65. Most respondents, moreover, disagreed with the statement that 'if people are very old and very ill their lives should not be prolonged by expensive treatment and the money should be spent elsewhere in the NHS'.

Public confusion about the problem may be attributable, in part, to ignorance. Most people in the survey had little idea of the cost of National Health Service (NHS) treatments. Nor were they very anxious to be enlightened by accountants. Asked who should establish NHS priorities, only 17 per cent said 'the general public', 14 per cent 'health service managers' and 9 per cent 'the Government'. The majority, nearly two-thirds, said 'doctors'.

Should doctors decide? Not everyone would agree; and various alternative prescriptions are on offer. In this chapter I shall look at three responses, proposed or in progress, to problems of health care rationing for the elderly:

1 The first response is that scarce or costly life-extending medical technologies should not be made available to people over a certain age. This has been openly advocated in the USA, but derives in part from American observation of something similar being done, rather less openly, in the British health service a decade or so ago.

2 The second response is in progress in the British health service now. Long-term care of frail elderly patients has been moved out of NHS hospitals (where care is publicly funded) into private nursing homes, where patients must 'spend down' their savings before they are eligible for support from public funds.

3 The third response is that of advocates of 'death with dignity'. Most of these want voluntary euthanasia to be decriminalised along lines pioneered in The Netherlands. But a few suggest that non-voluntary euthanasia for the demented might help solve the rationing problem.

Before examining these responses, however, I want to try to sketch a moral framework – related first to modern perceptions of old age and second to some older moral principles.

PERCEPTIONS OF OLD AGE: LITERARY

To readers of English literature, one of the best-known modern perceptions of old age is found in Philip Larkin's poem about the demented elderly, 'The Old Fools' (Larkin 1988). This powerful poem is a painful reminder of what old age may mean to many people today. It is, on three counts, a very modern poem. The first thing that makes it so modern is its tone of outrage:

> Do they somehow suppose
> It's more grown-up when your mouth hangs open and drools,
> And you keep on pissing yourself, and can't remember
> Who called this morning?
>
> (Larkin 1988)[1]

Shakespeare, for example, writes about

> second childishness and mere oblivion

104

Sans teeth, sans eyes, sans taste, sans everything.
(*As You Like It* II, 7: 165–6)

But Shakespeare seems to regard as a matter of course what Larkin protests against so strenuously. Shakespeare too, can write of the same subject in the first person.

Pray, do not mock me:
I am a very foolish fond old man,
Fourscore and upward, not an hour more or less;
And, to deal plainly,
I fear I am not in my perfect mind.
(*King Lear* IV, 7: 59–63)

In contrast, Larkin's perceptions are resolutely those of an observer, not a participant. That is the second thing that makes his poem so modern. The ambiguity of the poem's ending, which warns the reader that 'we' may yet 'find out' what 'the old fools' feel, indeed, is that 'we' may not 'find out': our days may outlast our insight; or we may, like the poet himself, die too soon. Either way, this suggests the observer's perspective will be the true one.

The third thing that makes 'The Old Fools' modern is its view of death, which Larkin alludes to as 'oblivion'. Oblivion, which Shakespeare located in subjectivity, here is objective, dead true. But this objectivity and the observer's view of dementia are purchased at the price already mentioned – that of outrage, of asking why 'the old fools' are not 'screaming' at the horror of their predicament.

The implication of Larkin's poem is that from a rational modern observer's point of view, screaming may be the only thing left when personally confronted with dementia. That, of course, was not Larkin's own way: his more controlled response was to write a poem about it. But in doing that he touched a modern raw nerve. If the life of a rational individual can end up like this, and if this modern view of death is correct, then a situation may have arisen 'to which the individual is incapable of adapting himself . . . and from which he begins to retreat', leading to 'a reanimation of modes of adaptation that belong to a period of childhood or infancy' (Nicoll 1918) – screaming, for example. Psychological regression, in other words, may be an inevitable side-effect of the modern objective observer's view of death and dementia.

Regression, I shall suggest later, may play a part in forming some current views of health care rationing for the elderly. But for now, let me not leave Larkin's rational observer without a further question.

How adequate is Larkin's modern view of death as oblivion? In particular, how adequate is this *modern* view, if we now live, as we are often told, in a *post-modern* age? Clearly, no-one is in a position to disprove it. But is it really the only alternative?

One alternative, which might fit better with the plethora of perspectives permitted in a post-modern age, is suggested by Kant. Death, he says (Kant [1794] 1983), can be thought of as the 'end of all time'. This thought, he claims, 'must be interwoven into human reason in a wonderful way, for it is found in one guise or another among all reasoning peoples in all times'. It is 'appealing . . . in part because of its obscurity, by which the imagination is made more powerfully active than by bright light'; and part of that obscurity for Kant, of course, is the paradox of thinking about 'no more time', when 'without the presupposition of time, nothing can be thought of'.

Obscure though it be, Kant's view of death seems less unsatisfactory, in a post-modern perspective, than Larkin's. Unlike 'oblivion', the 'end of all time' does not foreclose the question of what death is. It precludes, perhaps, the possibility that 'after death' (whatever that may mean) there is 'more of the same'. But otherwise it leaves open the possibility of anything from 'oblivion', through nirvana, to eternal life. Its only imperative, alike Kantian and post-modern, is that we do not try to silence our uncertainty by succumbing to metaphysical dogmatism, ancient or modern.

By much the same line of reasoning, I think, it is legitimate to question the rational modern observer's view of dementia. I don't want here to succumb to the cheerful clinician's assurance that many of his demented patients have never been so happy in their lives. But I doubt if the clinical poet's eye catches it either. Perspectives other than screaming red are possible – even if, like 'the end of all time', they may be obscure and paradoxical. What that possibility might mean is suggested, for example, in a more recent and no less powerful poem on the same subject, entitled simply 'Geriatric', by the octogenarian poet R. S. Thomas (Thomas 1995: 6).

PERCEPTIONS OF OLD AGE: ANTHROPOLOGICAL

The great majority of old people, however, are not and never will be demented. A post-modern view of them too need not be confined to a single socially problematic perspective. Their own experience has to be considered alongside what the non-elderly say about them. The latter, indeed, may tell us more about the non-elderly themselves than about the elderly. To elaborate this, let me turn to what the anthropologist Haim Hazan (1994) writes about how social scientists talk and society acts towards the elderly.

Hazan contrasts the position of the elderly in 'simple' (mostly traditional) and 'complex' (mostly modern) societies. In simple societies individuals are related to one another by multiple interwoven ties: familial, economic, religious and political. Growing old may mean becoming a wise leader of a pre-literate society or, in a subsistence-level society, being abandoned or ritually killed. But either way, there is a common understanding of what is going on. In complex societies, by contrast, individuals interact, often quite temporarily, in social groups which may have nothing to do with one another. Growing old often means being isolated: very old and needy individuals may end up disengaged from all but the single strand of a one-sided relationship with a bureaucratic agency, which sees them as 'problems'. Indeed, those in the mainstream of life may well see all those past the watershed of retirement as potential 'problems'. From the perspective of 'the pecuniary present', they are:

> non-productive and ... their contributions to and investments in society do not match the services and welfare they enjoy ... The aged are perceived as incapable of making any future returns, and any support rendered to them is deemed a matter of charity and not a right.
>
> (Hazan 1994: 19)

If they cannot or will not 'adapt' or 'adjust' to old age, or are past that possibility, moreover, the elderly may require 'handling', 'managing', 'organizing', 'looking after', 'caring for', 'placing' and 'planning' (Hazan 1994: 17).

This view of the elderly as actual or potential 'problems' (and indeed most academic or policy-oriented ways of categorising the elderly), Hazan argues, can be seen as 'a device for introducing order into an inherently ambiguous human condition'. Part of what makes old age ambiguous is that it is or often becomes, 'a state in which chronological time loses its grip over daily existence' (Hazan 1994: 72). In complex societies, the elderly find themselves isolated in a kind of limbo, where time and change do not indeed end, for their contemporaries are falling ill and dying daily; but where their previous experience in the mainstream of life cannot help them give meaning to, or exercise control over, their present existence.

Many old people learn to cope with this, Hazan observes, by 'divorcing the inner self from the outer self'. While 'the outer self continues to act and interact in the linear, culturally acceptable manner expected and rewarded by the social environment', the inner self creates 'an atemporal universe of meaning consisting of significant memories, tokens of cherished identity, and freely constructed life materials' (Hazan 1994: 84).

Hazan illustrates this by referring to 'the repetitive utterances of the elderly'. These need not signify mental decay or dementia – simply that the time-world of the elderly is disordered, at least from the point of view of the non-elderly. From the point of view of the elderly themselves, closer up to 'the end of all time', things may look different. This is suggested in a short story by Tracy Kidder, who describes an old man's thoughts on his even older nursing-home roommate's reminiscences.

> Local news was scant; around here a new story usually had to do with someone's new ailment. Lou's old stories were much more entertaining. Heard only twice, Lou's stories could seem monotonous. Heard many times, they were like old friends. They were comforting. Lou's memories seemed like an immortal part of him. They existed right now forever. Lou's memories contained such a density of life that in their presence death seemed impossible.
>
> (Kidder 1993: 46)

That last interpretative reference to death may or may not be in place. It is interpreted, remember, by a story-writer, an observer; and Hazan may be right to suspect that 'meaningful communication with the old can take place only among the old' (Hazan 1994: 86). He observes, moreover, that although most old people are in no hurry to die, the evidence suggests that they fear death much less than do the middle aged (Hazan 1994: 72). The middle aged's view of the old as a mass of problems, indeed, may be a way of distancing death by distancing 'them'. In subsistence-level societies, distancing 'may take the form of the actual physical destruction of the elderly, usually with their consent', because the elderly themselves recognise that they are an insupportable economic burden. But in 'societies of relative abundance', where sheer physical survival is no longer the issue, the elderly still may be distanced, and regardless of their consent, primarily to serve the psychological needs of the non-elderly. In these societies, the form distancing takes 'may mean not only preserving the physical bodies of the aged but often sustaining them with elaborate medical care' (Hazan 1994: 27).

MORAL PRINCIPLES

Distancing the elderly, isolating them physically and conceptually, and ultimately preserving and sustaining their socially dead bodies – these, Hazan suggests, may be 'devices for introducing order into an inherently ambiguous human condition'. For whose benefit? These, surely, are the psychological regressive responses of grown-up children, unwilling to adapt to losing a parental buffer between themselves and death. The motives of the middle aged, indeed, may be even darker. But if we want moral principles to guide rationing, suffice it to say that these regressive responses go against one of the greatest: 'Act in such a way that you always treat humanity, whether in your own person or in the person of any other, never simply as a means, but always at the same time as an end' (Kant [1785] 1948).

Even Kant, of course, finally succumbed to dementia – but not before cheerfully practising what he preached in his 'regimen for prolonging man's life' (Kant [1798] 1992), and also doing much of his best work late in life. Others of his moral rules also remain relevant. An example, with distancing still in mind, is what he writes (Kant [1797] 1991: 244) about the 'principle of *mutual love*', which 'admonishes men constantly to *come closer* to one another' and the principle of 'the *respect* they owe one another, to keep themselves *at a distance* from one another': 'should one of these great moral forces fail', Kant warns, moral chaos will ensue.

Love and respect, in Kant's book, are not 'mere' feelings, but maxims, yardsticks of how we should conduct ourselves toward one another. Respect is an exceptionless duty – not to do anything that violates the 'dignity of humanity in another person'. The requirements of love may be more difficult to assign: but it is still a duty – 'to promote according to one's means the happiness of others in need' (Kant [1797] 1991: 247). These two principles, surely, provide the best short summary we are likely to find, of how grown-ups, of whatever age, should equilibrate their mutual relationships. So what, if we take them to heart, are the implications for health care rationing?

RATIONING HEALTH CARE

To answer this, first a little more may need to be said about rationing. Rationing is usually believed to be necessary when rising expectations have to be met from limited resources, and when leaving the outcome to market forces is thought to be unjust or socially harmful. In such circumstances, rationing is often seen as the most rational response. Yet this is, arguably, a modern perspective and also a problematic one.

Historically, the rationality of rationing derives from emergency contexts, particularly those of modern warfare, in which providing the same fixed amount of food to each soldier or horse (their 'rations') is justified by military necessity. In the same context however, health care resources are allocated not on this equal shares basis, but by triage, which treats dissimilar cases differently, on the basis of individual medical need and the likelihood of medical success. Claims for the rationality of rationing in health care resource allocation thus exist in tension with (traditionally more influential) claims based on triage rationality; and while rationing is sometimes defended on the grounds that it is a more rational way of allocating resources to groups or populations than is triage (which is concerned with choosing between individuals), this somewhat artificial distinction is often difficult to sustain in practice.

Rationing itself is particularly hard to justify when the possibilities of medical progress are expanding, living standards rising, and the policies of democratic governments coming under increasing public scrutiny. In this context, public agreement on the need for rationing, let alone on the best form for it to take, is not easy to achieve. Today, the modern hope that problems of health care resource allocation could be solved by public acceptance of rational rationing systems devised by governments or bureaucrats seems to be foundering. An alternative, when public opinion does not allow governments to abdicate responsibility to market forces, is a more post-modern hope – that a process of informed public debate on the issues may lead to sufficient agreement on the least unsatisfactory procedures by which health care resources can be distributed in the least unfair ways.

With these considerations in mind, let me return to the three rationing responses I mentioned at the outset.

RATIONING RESPONSES: 1

The first rationing response is that scarce or costly life-extending technologies should not be available to people over a certain age. Age in itself is an insufficient predictor of likely medical benefit (overall health status is the relevant criterion): so presumably that is not the reason for proposing this, unless we are being regressively simplistic. Norman Daniels' 'prudential life-span' argument (Daniels 1985), however, is more subtle. He asks us to imagine:

1 That we want the best cooperative scheme to cover our own 'health, family, and economic eventualities over a lifetime'. As prudent deliberators, our aim is a scheme which gives us a fair chance of enjoying the normal range of opportunities for each stage of our lives.
2 That while deliberating about this we are ignorant of our own actual 'age, family situation, health status, and genetic history, socioeconomic status or . . . particular conception of the good' (Daniels 1985:103).
3 That we then have to consider two rationing schemes:

> Scheme A involves a direct appeal to an age criterion: no one over age 70 is eligible to receive any of several high-cost, life-extending technologies. . . . Because age rationing greatly reduces the utilization of each technology, there are resources available for developing all of them. . . .
> Scheme B rejects age rationing and allocates life extending technology solely by medical need, As a result, it can either develop just one such technology, say dialysis, making it available to anyone who needs it, or it can develop several and ration them by lottery.
>
> (Daniels 1985: 91)

Scheme A, Daniels argues, offers everyone a higher chance of achieving the normal life-span, whereas B offers a higher chance of living beyond the normal life-span only to those lucky enough to reach it. So prudent deliberators would choose A, since 'prudence would dictate giving greater emphasis to enhancing individual chances of reaching a normal lifespan than to extending the normal lifespan' (Daniels 1985: 106). Scheme A, moreover, is not only prudent, but fair, because 'it works through time: *each* of us, not

111

just a particular group of people, will enjoy the increased chance of reaching the normal lifespan under A' (Daniels 1985: 107).

Daniels' defence of age-based rationing, which I have sketched only in bare outline, seems in principle a fair and reasonable response to the American predicament – namely, the steadily increasing proportion of the health care budget spent on scarce and expensive medical technologies to prolong the last few years of elderly patients' lives. In principle, it respects the elderly, because it applies to all individuals equally – each in their generation has an equal chance of enjoying the normal range of opportunities for each stage of their lives. In principle too, it recognises the duty to promote the happiness of others according to one's means: means are not infinite and others also include the non-elderly.

In practice, however, the argument has problems. These include unfairness to the initial elderly generation involved, and the perennial worry that savings here may not actually be used better there. But they also include the more basic issue of context. As Daniels himself points out, his argument shows only that age-based rationing (unlike sex-based or race-based rationing) *can* be defensible. The crucial conditions are 1) whether it is 'part of a basic institution that distributes resources over the lifetime of the individuals it affects' (i.e. not piecemeal age rationing by individual doctors or hospitals), and 2) whether the 'basic institutions' of the society in which it operates 'comply with acceptable principles of distributive justice'. In a society where the 'worst off among the elderly are usually the same people who were worst off in earlier stages of their lives', he says, 'rationing by age could make things even worse' (Daniels 1985: 111–13).

RATIONING RESPONSES: 2

Similar caveats apply to the recent British shift in the locus of long-term care from publicly funded hospitals to means-tested nursing homes. As noted earlier, the American debate gained some impetus from observation (Aaron and Schwartz 1984) of how rationing scarce and expensive life-extending technologies by age served to contain costs in the British health service a decade or so ago. At this time a crucial gatekeeping role was played by general practitioners, who often hesitated to send old people to hospital for the kind of treatment they might get (if they could afford it) in the USA, partly because the GPs knew that hospital resources were limited, but also because they knew that hospital treatment might prolong these patients' lives for only a brief and perhaps unhappy time.

GPs, of course, had to use their clinical judgement before reaching the conclusion that 'not much could be done' by sending the patient to hospital. But when that verdict was delivered and continuing home care offered, most elderly British patients tended to accept it. They did so, although they might not have put it in those terms, more or less along the lines of Daniels' argument: the NHS had served them well, but younger people would probably benefit more from its scarce hospital resources. Their own doctor, moreover, had nothing to gain from advising them one way or the other, and so his advice could be trusted.

Today, things have changed – perhaps as a result of GP fund-holding, certainly with the growth in the elderly proportion of the population and the cost of health care. But for the purpose of the present discussion, two things seem clear.

1 NHS hospital wards are not necessarily the most efficient or effective places for long-term care of the frail but not acutely ill elderly: a nursing home may provide just as good care as a long-stay geriatric ward; and good nursing-home care costs less than good hospital care.

2 The growing cost of providing all health care for the frail elderly from the public purse may require either higher taxes or cuts in other public spending. If that is not politically acceptable, an alternative may be to abandon universal benefits and introduce means-testing, requiring better-off old people (or their families) to contribute to their own care.

Given these considerations, the British means-testing response might seem fair and reasonable, especially from a government democratically elected on a manifesto promising to reduce taxes. Why should the elderly not accept means-testing from the government much as they once accepted the GPs' advice?

Again, things are more complicated. In principle, both a shift in the locus of long-term care and the introduction of some form of means-testing might have been justified. What is more difficult to justify was using the former to bring about the latter in a form that discriminated unfairly against a particularly vulnerable section of the population. In practice, the new policy meant that if elderly patients needed acute medical care, this would be paid for from public funds: but if they needed long-term nursing care, the state would begin to pay for this only when the patient's own resources were less than £8,000 (later raised to £16,000).

As a result of this new national health lottery, many old people of modest means, who had paid taxes and national insurance contributions on the understanding that this would provide a 'cradle to grave NHS', now found that they had to use up their savings and sell their homes to pay for expensive nursing-home care in the last few months of their lives. That might have been morally defensible, of course, had it been what every generation had experienced, and had all in the present generation been in the same boat. But the latter was not true of old people who had sufficient capital invested to provide income to pay their nursing-home costs. Requiring those with small savings to 'spend down' before receiving state support, thus could only increase the growth in inequality as well as in poverty evident in recent decades (Le Grand 1993).

Even that, of course, might be defended (politically if not morally) as a regrettable necessity, if necessity it were. But that is far from clear. The popular argument for cutting state expenditure on the elderly relies on the notion of a growing proportion of old people depending on a dwindling proportion of productive younger people. But even after further expected growth of the elderly population in the new century, 'by 2041, four fifths of the population will still be aged below 65' (Le Grand 1993). Against this background there seems more than a whiff of psychological regression in talk about public spending on the frail elderly getting 'out of control'. This suspicion, indeed, has recently received confirmation from an all-party committee of the British House of Commons, which forthrightly criticised the means-testing scheme and argued 'that much of the speculation about a crisis was founded on unsound evidence or was "downright alarmist" (*The Times* 1996).

Criticism of this covert attempt to introduce means-testing, of course, does not lead to the conclusion that there are no limits to the amount of health care that can be provided from public funds. Morally, the pertinent question may be the one Coleridge asked: 'What matters it to a man, that he pays six times more Taxes than his father did, if, notwithstanding, he with the same portion of exertion enjoys twice the comforts which his father did?' (Coleridge [1818] 1969).

But, politically, the electorate need to be convinced of such obvious truths, and in the current political climate that is far from easy. Given the tendency of health care costs to rise with rising popular expectations, difficult decisions about priorities will always need to be made. But the need for such decisions, and the fairness of the form they take, will have to be openly demonstrated – not least to those who will bear the personal as well as the financial consequences.

Demonstrating this is especially difficult in an allegedly post-modern age, when many argue that all moral perspectives are relative and deference to authority is in short supply. Yet even in this context, public support for 'tough choices' is more likely to be gained if 'the basic institutions' of society are perceived 'to comply with the principles of distributive justice'. In this context too, if most people do indeed believe that doctors should establish NHS priorities, that traditional trust in a basic institution should not be sniffed at by the hard nosed. Part of the message of post-modernity may be that moral traditions are more enduring than modernity assumed; and that, variable across space, they are malleable in time, and can be constructively moulded by sensitive hands.

RATIONING RESPONSES: 3

For the present purpose, a brief reference to the third response mentioned at the outset may suffice. To suggest euthanasia as an answer to 'the problem of the elderly' is regression with a vengeance. There are circumstances (however rare) in which *voluntary* euthanasia can be morally justified. But they do not include those of frail and not very well-off people, with the prospect of public policy impoverishing them, being tempted to seek an early death in order to have something left to hand on to their children or grandchildren. That may well be the main reason to reject, for the time being, decriminalisation of voluntary euthanasia in Britain.

As to the future, it may be instructive to enquire, for example, not just about the practice of euthanasia in The Netherlands, but also about how its practice is interwoven with that country's democratic institutions, welfare provision and doctor-patient relationships. The nature of such basic institutions, and the state of mind of those who operate them, rather than the details of specific rationing schemes, may be the crucial moral factor. The heart of ethics beats, not in actions, but in agents. Do they observe the spirit as well as the letter of Kant's 'maxim of common interest'? Are the elderly 'to be considered fellow men [and women], that is, rational beings with needs, united by nature in one dwelling place so that they can help one another' (Kant [1797] 1991: 247)?

THE ETHICS OF HEALTH CARE MANAGEMENT

What implications has this discussion of age-based rationing in a post-modern world for the broader theme of this book – the ethics of health care management? I have not attempted to define 'post-modern' – a term used in different ways by different people. But part of what it points to is a growing awareness that 'rational solutions' to 'social problems', devised by experts and implemented by officials, are likely to be more elusive than was often assumed in the modern era of recent centuries; and that while choices and decisions about the allocation of scarce resources will always be needed, their effectiveness and efficiency will increasingly depend on public perception of how they are made and by whom.

In the ethics of health care generally, this means that attention needs to be paid not only to moral principles and casuistry, but also to procedural and 'virtue' ethics. In the ethics of medical practice, the evident shift from an ethos of paternalism to one of partnership and shared decision-making with patients is a useful pointer to how larger problems in the political economy of health care might be tackled more constructively. The management of health care, like the management of individual patients, is more likely to succeed when the interdependence of those who are, for the time being, agents and those who are, for the time being, patients is acknowledged, and when decisions are reached through open discussion and mutual empowerment.

NOTE

1   'The Old Fools' from *Collected Poems* (1988) by Philip Larkin reprinted by kind permission of Faber and Faber Ltd.

BIBLIOGRAPHY

Aaron, H. J. and Schwartz, W. B. (1984) *The Painful Prescription*, Washington DC: The Brookings Institution.

Coleridge, S. T. [1818] (1969) 'On the vulgar errors respecting taxes and taxation', first published in B. E. Rooke (ed.), *The Friend*, in *Collected Works*, 1, 4, London: Routledge, p. 237.

Daily Telegraph (1994) 'Rationing health care: who should come first?', Monday 12 September: 5.

Daniels, N. (1985) *Just Health Care*, Cambridge: CUP.

Hazan, H. (1994) *Old Age: Constructions and Deconstructions*, Cambridge: CUP.

Kant, I. [1785] (1948) *Groundwork of the Metaphysic of Morals* trans. H. J. Paton in *The Moral Law*, London: Hutchinson.

—— [1794] (1983) 'The end of all things', trans. T. Humphrey in *Perpetual Peace and Other Essays*, Indianapolis: Hacket.

—— [1797] (1991) *The Metaphysics of Morals*, trans. M. Gregor, Cambridge: CUP.

—— [1798] (1992) *The Conflict of the Faculties*, trans. M. J. Gregor, Lincoln NE: University of Nebraska Press.

Kidder, T. (1993) 'The last place on earth', *Granta* 44: 10–48.

Larkin, P. (1988) 'The Old Fools' in *Collected Poems*, London: Faber and Faber.

Le Grand, J. (1993) 'Can we afford the welfare state?', *British Medical Journal* 307: 1018–19.

Nicoll, M. (1918) 'The conception of regression in psychological medicine', *The Lancet* 9 June: 797–8.

Shakespeare, W. [1600] (1957) *As You Like It* in W. J. Craig (ed.), *Complete Works of Shakespeare*, Oxford: OUP.

—— [1605] (1957) *King Lear* in W. J. Craig (ed.), *Complete Works of Shakespeare*, Oxford: OUP.

The Times (1996) 'Age time bomb is alarmist myth, MPs tell ministers', Thursday 8 August: 2.

Thomas, R. S. (1995) *No Truce with the Furies*, Newcastle-uponTyne: Bloodaxe Books, p. 9.

7

HEALTH CARE IN POLAND

Dilemmas of transformation

Jacek Holówka

In this chapter I intend to describe challenges that Polish health care services face at present, and draw some more general conclusions from the Polish example.

Until 1989 most medical services in Poland were provided by a nationalised health care system, which offered them at no direct cost to the patient. Medical care was covered from the state budget. Over the past decades, however, the system became more and more inefficient, bureaucratic and mismanaged. Its demise was triggered by the fall of communism. Since 1990 numerous private clinics have emerged alongside state clinics, and the two kinds of institutions immediately create a strange contrast. The old establishments still operate on the lofty principle of universal coverage, supported by the universal right of every individual to receive full medical assistance irrespective of their ability to pay. The new clinics consider medical skills one more kind of marketable commodity and make their services available to those who are ready to pay their full price only. A person in need of medical care has two rather unattractive options to choose from.

First, she may present herself at a local health care institution supported from public funds and require help. She will pay nothing, or almost nothing, but she will have to wait before a doctor sees her, and when he eventually does, she will meet a physician who is overworked and underpaid. The doctor will not question the lofty ideals on which his institution has been founded, but neither will he degrade its mission by trying to accommodate the mundane needs of his patient, such as the desire to be served promptly and competently. He will either send her home after a brief examination with one or two prescriptions in her hand, or he will refer her to another practitioner, preferably a specialist. This treatment meets with mixed feelings. Public clinics offer little comfort but much security. They throw nobody into the streets and their professional standards are, as a rule, adequate. In the case of a serious condition, their services can be superb, definitely unmatched by anything that private institutions can offer. The latter cannot afford to install advanced diagnostic equipment or to build well-equipped operation rooms. However, access to public institutions is severely limited. The patient may have to wait for more than a year for an elective operation or several months for an expensive laboratory test. Some patients console themselves by the thought that the system is in principle egalitarian and offers services of the same quality to everybody, irrespective of their ability to pay. This offers them a strong sense of security.

Second, the patient may decide to go to a private clinic. She will get a prompt and competent service, but she will have to pay a high fee and – unless she is well on her guard – she may be turned into a chronic case, heavily dependent on her doctor. The doctor will be a well-trained practitioner and not ostensibly greedy, but she will find ways of tempting her to use her services more widely. In general, private clinics are more sensitive to the patients' anxieties and their desire to get well. Their staff are supportive and gentle and, for a certain category of patients, this friendliness, rather than egalitarianism, is essential for their sense of well-being.

The contrast between the two styles of medical assistance indicates that, ideally, a health care system should satisfy at least two sets of demands:

1 It should be accessible to all, irrespective of the patient's ability to pay and, preferably, it should be free. Free services alleviate the fear of conflict between health care and other important life plans. Families are spared the necessity of deciding, for example, which is more important for them: providing for the education of the younger generation or for medical assistance to ageing parents. Most families cannot do both, if both health and education must be paid from their private accounts.

2 A health care system should provide help promptly and make the patient feel comfortable. The patient should be able to communi-

cate with the doctor easily and should feel confident that some-body will monitor the progress of therapy and offer all necessary advice. Thus, clinics should inspire trust by providing patients with full information about their cases and by not discouraging further contacts.

It is extremely difficult, however, to create a system of health care that has the merits of nationalised and private medicine at the same time. This is especially hard in a well-educated society that is informed about new methods of medical treatment, life-supporting systems, transplantation procedures, etc. A real difficulty arises when the average level of expectation addressed to the health care system are higher than the average ability to pay. The gap is exacer-bated if nationalised medicine legitimises health care expectations, without being able to satisfy them, and private medicine delegiti-mates the expectations, while offering good quality services only to the rich few. The public is then divided into customers of state insti-tutions and customers of private institutions, and the two groups ogle one another with envy and suspicion.

The complementarity of the two systems (egalitarianism vs friendliness) leads some people to believe that a mix of the two could produce a satisfactory situation: if only the people who can wait choose state medicine, and those who can pay choose private clinics; if those who have to educate their children use the national system, and those who have no children to educate send their parents to private institutions; etc. In fact, the dividing lines cannot be drawn so neatly. Most families are made up of young and old people, and most families are neither prepared to cover high costs of medical services when the need for the expense arises suddenly, nor can they wait if an urgent case develops. Thus, having the two systems side by side produces more negative than positive effects, a lot of friction and little synergy. The contrast generates frustration in the private institutions and breeds corruption in the public ones. It gives bad consciences to doctors who charge high fees in private clinics and it demoralises public hospitals which increasingly try to incorporate some of the financial practices that are used in the private sector. Moreover, a situation is created where some health needs are simply not met by either kind of institution. Some patients find it impossible either to wait or to pay, and then they have nowhere to go. Or almost nowhere. In an effort to answer their needs a third type of health care covertly develops – a dilettante practice, a mixture of folk medicine, herbal treatment, quaint diets, experiments with over-the-counter drugs and oriental medicine. This alternative medicine is fostered by quack doctors, local half-wits, people possessing a small library of self-help manuals, and compassionate midwives. It is difficult to judge how widespread this practice is, as no research has been conducted to reveal its scope. But one can often find press advertisements for such services, which indicates that it is a growing industry.

It appears then that we can roughly identify three kinds of medical help in Poland: nationalised medicine, private practice and home-grown unprofessional self-help. Each has its own merits and faults. The first is egalitarian and free, but mismanaged and slow; the second is professional and supportive but costly and highly selective; the third is inexpensive and friendly, but dangerously unscientific and potentially harmful.

Although it is risky to generalise in this context, I would be tempted to say that the difficulties that nationalised medicine has been encountering in Poland are not unique to the Polish case. Any country that has tried a system of nationalised health care either has already faced, or will face, similar difficulties. The ideal of universal coverage is so alluring, however, that even when all the difficulties associated with it are recognised, it is still generally favoured, the hope always being that sufficient resources will be somehow generated to support it. However, after a glorious beginning, nationalised medicine is usually forced to introduce heavy bureaucratic constraints that work for a short time and then prove entirely ineffective. Sooner or later, nationalised medicine is supplemented by private and/or unprofessional practice.

In view of the discussion so far I feel justified in offering a comparison between the two systems that are fully developed in Poland, nationalised and private medicine, and a remote example of health care in South Africa, where folk healing has developed almost to the complete satisfaction of the local population. I cannot imagine a similar system finding acceptance anywhere in Europe, but as a clear type it is very instructive. Its elements are ever more pronounced in Poland, where, for instance, the public was recently alarmed to hear of the number of births that have taken place secretly outside professional clinics which were followed by infanticide. Apparently, while abortion was illegal in Poland (until late 1996), several women used the secret services of self-appointed midwives and perpetrated crime. More importantly, folk medicine points to something that is indispensable in every form of health care, but often overlooked – social acceptance. It is interesting that social acceptance can be dissociated from both moral considerations and scientific standards. Whenever this happens unprofessional medicine finds good conditions to grow.

Some of the issues that arise from the considerations above I wish to discuss in this chapter. More specifically I will consider: 1) how a traditional, folk medicine that is completely unscientific but perfectly integrated with the entire social culture, offers a counterpart to modern medicine; 2) how a nationalised system of health care that offers equality can be overburdened and paralysed by the growing demands of the public; 3) how private medicine that is highly efficient but driven by profit rather than other motives leaves many health needs unanswered; and 4) how a 'third party' system, based on the idea of an independent, non-government agency commissioned to purchase health care services for the population from the providers of these services, promises to combine all the requisite advantages as a *universally accessible, reasonably financed, scientifically sound* and *socially acceptable* organisation of health care. I will show the four systems side by side in Table 7.1, at the end of this chapter, where their presumed advantages are compared in more detail. The comparison will make clear, I hope, what additional values underlie the four systems. I do not believe that it is possible to say how important each of these values is for a satisfactory distribution of health services. But they seem to offer some idea of what is wrong with systems that meet only narrowly defined expectations of some specific professional or social and political groups.

I will argue that the 'third party' system has a certain remarkable quality that is not shared by the remaining systems. When it deteriorates, it does not remain generically the same, but turns into one of the three inferior systems: nationalised, private or unscientific medicine. The other three do not possess such propensity. When they decline, they remain in the same category, and become simply a worse version of themselves. This unusual quality of the 'third party' system recommends it as something simultaneously precious and fragile.

HEALING AS A SOCIAL RITUAL

Societies that offer scientifically deficient medical practices can develop amazingly strong doctor-patient relationships, marked by trust and mutual understanding. A case in point is Bomvanaland in South Africa. The local system of medicine, based on custom rather than science, incorporates a sensible conception of disease, clearly determines the roles of the patient and the healer and engages the whole family in the care of the patient.

> On the day agreed upon the patient and his company walk in a single file all the way to visit the diviner selected. . . . Having arrived at the place of the diviner, they enter the hut of the seance and sit down in a half circle. The acolytes of the diviner start singing and clapping their hands and thus create an atmosphere of loaded tension and expectancy. When the diviner starts the consultation he begins by guessing. He is not supposed to take 'the medical history' by interviewing the patient and/or his relatives. On the contrary, he is the one who gives the answers to all the questions about the patient and the causes of his disease.
>
> (Jansen 1973: 43)

The indigenous medicine of Bomvanaland produces diagnoses in a close interaction between the diviner and the family of the patient. The diviner assembles the visitors and the patient together with his assistants, and proceeds to guess the symptoms of the disease. If he makes a right guess, the audience confirms his finding with sounds of approval. If he makes a mistake they sound displeasure. The diviner is never discomfited by criticism but simply announces: 'I lied'. This bold statement is invariably greeted with much admiration. The family is relieved. The healer they have found not only demonstrates a profound understanding of the case but also tests their alertness and their knowledge of the patient's condition. In this way mutual confidence is established, confirmed and cemented. The diviner finds his audience attentive and watchful, they find him competent and critical. A sense of partnership develops and the process of healing, which engages all the abilities of the healer, his assistants and the visitors, is at that moment initiated.

The case history is constructed more and more completely, and the interview gradually passes into a trance that engulfs the healer, his assistants and the family of the patient. Through incantations and rhythmical motions the group acquires a sense of understanding of the nature of the disease. At some point, in unanimity, they discover that they can cope with the disease. The consultation comes to a close. No verbal diagnosis is pronounced, no medications

123

are offered. The group wins some sort of understanding and goes home. After a few days either the patient gets better or he does not. If he does get better, the family sends an ox to the diviner as a reward for the service. If the patient dies, the healer receives nothing, as manifestly he has rendered no service of value.

This interesting arrangement solves most of the intractable issues of health care management, although it is based on nothing more than a strict observance of a number of cultural rituals: there is one price for every service, the health profession is protected from being flooded by patients with minor ailments, the presence of assistants motivates the healer to do his best, the participation of the entire family confirms the credibility of the ritual and creates motivation for the best care of the patient.

It is quite obvious that the system has a glaring deficiency stemming from inadequate knowledge of scientific medicine. The healer has no conception of human biology and no use for effective medication. He does not administer any treatment but simply inspires faith. Moreover, the scope of health care services is limited. No pro-health practices are promoted, no medical education is offered to acolytes, minor ailments remain completely unattended to. But even with these unquestionable shortcomings the medical system of Bomvanaland is amazingly well integrated with the basic cultural norms of the society and remarkably efficient in translating a biological problem into one that can be solved by a socially prescribed ritual.

BARRIERS AND DISCONTINUITIES

It is interesting to notice that one cannot preserve the merits of a socially accepted system of health care, like the one that exists in Bomvanaland, and at the same time correct its various faults, such as the inability to provide scientifically sound treatment. Health care systems are not amenable to piecemeal changes. Suppose that someone contemplates introducing scientific methods to the Bomvanaland system, while preserving the rest of the system intact. This may be a foreign visitor who wishes to get the best of both worlds – keep an admirable culture and modernise services. Can such a gentle reformer ever be successful? She may offer rudimentary medical training to the practising diviners; she may teach them basic anatomy, hygiene and pharmacy; she may introduce them to human physiology and explain to them something about the nature of basic diseases; she may provide them with basic medications and teach them about methods of efficient treatment. Let us further suppose that the healers are responsive to these overtures and learn the essentials. Thus they may find it expedient at the end of a traditional consultation to offer their visitors biologically active medications.

For a while nothing very much will change. But sooner or later some questions are likely to be asked. For example: 'Why should we continue with the trance and incantations?' or 'What is the use of having so many assistants?'. The families of the patient may come to wonder why they should continue to make troublesome trips, go into trance and decide collectively what should be done, if what really counts in the end is a bottle of medicine. They may lose faith in the traditional methods and rely on chemicals instead. They may find it difficult to believe that the disease is sent by a vicious neighbour or that it develops in the patient's liver as a result of someone's jealousy. They may instead come to believe in germs and happily gobble Aspirin, antibiotics and pain killers. The healer may eventually be perceived as a half-trained quack doctor who plays with the life and limb of his patients without having any appropriate knowledge. His basic skills may no longer find any audience. He may no longer be invited to perform the traditional rituals. The ill person may prefer to seek advice from a licensed doctor nearby. The healer may soon realise that he is another victim of changing times. He may find it difficult to understand that his own deficient education is to blame. After all, has he not learned a lot lately? How could he have been popular while he knew nothing of foreign medicine and have lost his reputation now that he has acquired some knowledge of it? Perhaps his teachers are his enemies; otherwise they would not have deprived him of his living and his reputation by bringing in foreigners who take his customers away from him. He may want to fight back. But all that he may be able to do will be to revert to incantations, trance, group consultations. It is unlikely that these methods will bring him his old patients back, so he may resort to coaxing, pleading and threatening in order to discourage his kinsmen from seeing the licensed doctors. He may spread gossip and innuendoes to the effect that there are more diseases now than there were while no foreign doctors were around. He may accuse the foreigners of having an evil eye, of selling bottles with dangerous germs, etc. Whether he succeeds or not, the fact remains that the healer who works like a physician will never become a member of the traditional system of medicine. Licensed doctors and healers cannot work side by side, even if the latter adopt some of the methods of their licensed counterparts. Scientific education creates a discontinuity in the traditional system and precipitates its ruin.

It is not difficult to understand why this should be so. In a sense, every system of health care is like an organism that relies on internal connections and interdependencies. For instance, once the roles of the providers and the customers in a system are defined, some forms of payment are not acceptable. A modern doctor will not accept an ox, a traditional healer will have little use for £5. If the specific connections and interdependencies are broken, the system disintegrates. This is as much true of Bomvanaland as of Poland. A failing system cannot be repaired by a foreign implant – foreign in the functional sense of the term. Two systems cannot be improved upon by a merger that could compensate for their partial faults. If you have a system fuelled by a highly idealistic notion of the physician's obligation to help the patient, it would be incongruous to allow in it the element of fee for service. If the system makes use of modern and efficient technology, it would be incongruous to expect that the whole family of the patient is involved in the making of a diagnosis or in the creating of a therapeutic environment. Various components of a health care system interrelate and must dovetail. So even if a system has only one feature that is highly questionable, for example if it does not incorporate the scientific approach, it cannot be saved by attaching, so to speak, the desirable property, while leaving everything else unchanged. The principle of functionalism that prohibits exchanging parts between sufficiently dissimilar wholes seems to hold good in health care, whether or not it holds good generally in anthropology or sociology. For this reason you cannot reform a nationalised health care system by introducing partial insurance and you cannot obliterate the economic motivation of private clinics by inviting them to offer occasional free medical check-ups to some mountain villagers or to boy scouts. If a health care system needs to be reformed, it usually needs to be rebuilt from the beginning. Or at least it can resemble a church in Rome, where some Roman stones have been used to construct a clearly non-Roman place of worship.

HOPES OF UNIVERSAL COVERAGE

The idea of starting from scratch was implemented after World War II when a national health care system was created in Great Britain, and similar systems of nationalised health care were introduced in many countries of Central and Eastern Europe. These systems were quite popular at first. The war had just ended and it seemed appropriate that the veterans, who only a few years ago had risked their lives, should now be treated free of charge, and that similar services should be offered to their families or, for that matter, to anyone who needed them. The sense of a new social bond was created, and free access to health institutions was perceived as a human right. Those who fell ill were no longer left to their own resources but could count on others. The system of private medical practice based on the principle of fee for service seemed obsolete in this new context.

> past trends indicate the ... ultimate form that a health-services system and methods of paying for it would take if there were no countervailing forces ... all health services would be completely tax supported according to a graduated income tax so that the higher-income families would pay more than the lower-income families; all health services would be provided at no direct charge to anyone; all facilities would be owned by the government; all health personnel would be salaried; and all curative and preventive services ... would be available.
>
> (Anderson 1972: 288)

Undoubtedly national health care systems had many advantages: they offered well-designed medical services to everyone who needed them and advanced a concern for the patient; organisation of professional practice, payment for services, health care administration plus several preventive pro-health activities were all subsumed under one system of decision-making (very often supervised by a central ministry of health); from the organisational as well as from the moral point of view, disease and disability were no longer private calamities but social problems of high priority to be handled by powerful state organisations; infirmity aroused sympathy and the will to help; patients felt welcome in health care institutions where they confidently required medical assistance.

It was observed quite early, however, that these systems had promised more than they could deliver. Initially, when sophisticated

127

equipment was not in wide use and the countries of Europe were busy repairing their war damages, the idea of offering health care to anyone in need seemed credible. At that time government programmes focused on the prevention of contagious diseases, such as tuberculosis, or on acute conditions and on emergencies. Other medical problems – unless they severely limited the functioning of the patient – were de-emphasised. This restrictive policy was not applied consistently, however, as it was increasingly difficult to draw a line between incapacitating and discomforting conditions. More and more patients presented themselves with nothing more than the symptoms of ageing, stress or adverse consequences of unhealthy lifestyles. To reduce the growing demand for health services some countries used clauses eliminating, for example, frequent replacement of eye glasses or dental care from their health care systems. Other countries kept large segments of their populations out of the system. For instance, Polish peasants, who constituted more than half of the entire population, were not included in the nationalised health care system from the outset on the grounds that, as private producers, they did not contribute directly to the creation of the national product and consequently did not deserve to profit from the benefits of socialism.

This barrier was not popular in Poland and was moreover patently incompatible with the moral justification of universal coverage. Besides, it could be surmounted effortlessly. If the father in an average peasant family took part-time employment in any state enterprise, his entire family became automatically eligible for health care services. However, the fact that practically everyone was eventually covered by health insurance did not worry the ruling party. After all, the rural population was attracted to towns, which meant that cheap labour was offered to developing industry and that the size of the non-socialist sector was shrinking. The communist regime wanted to bring the entire society under a single system of administration. Health administration was a good starting point, as the process was spontaneous and eagerly approved of by those concerned. But the economic and social costs of the transition were enormous. Agricultural production fell, industry lagged behind and the socialist amenities very soon proved to be too scarce to go around.

In order to cope with the growing burdens of the health care system, new specialised clinics were created for those segments of the population which were vital for the integrity of the political system, i.e. for the miners, the military, employees of central state offices, etc. The clinics were given state of the art equipment and sufficient funds to keep up high standards. By the same token, however, the remaining clinics found themselves further disadvantaged, as they had to face growing pressure from patients who did not work in the politically relevant institutions. All the same, the idea of free medical care was not questioned, and as long as access to clinics, although often difficult, was not completely blocked – as indeed it has never been to this day – the failing system was considered the best possible solution in the difficult times of postwar, or post-postwar, reconstruction. Exiles from Eastern Europe and the Soviet Union, when they found a haven in the West, still had fond memories of the health care systems of their countries of origin, even if they considered the systems inefficient.

> the émigrés had experienced, in the course of their lifetime, at least two basic types of medical systems: 'third-party'[1] medicine in the Soviet Union ... and 'fee-for-service' medicine in the United States. They were therefore in a fairly good position to make comparative judgements and evaluations *qua* patients ... 73 per cent of the respondents, when specifically asked which system of medical care they preferred, opted in favor of the Soviet system over the American. The reason they adduced was that in the Soviet Union, however inadequate medical care had been, they at least had a legitimate claim to it, not as charity, but as a right spelled out in the Constitution.
>
> (Field 1972: 223)

The situation changed when the period of reconstruction was over and European societies were eager to experience new prosperity for all. In communist countries these hopes soared higher than elsewhere, as all daily miseries had been justified for years by the claim that huge resources were used for collective consumption. An average worker could not buy a car, a television set or live in a decent house, but he expected free education for his children, interesting holidays by the sea and convenient city transportation. First and foremost, however, he expected full medical care for his entire family. But it became increasingly clear that medical care was not as all-encompassing as was expected. The blame was put on a failing economy, and rightly so. The country as a whole produced too little to offer higher standards of living to everyone and all-encompassing medical services. The government became determined to take measures to improve the sluggish economy. So, for example, state companies were permitted to introduce 'financial incentives'. In addition to their monthly salaries workers were now paid bonuses in sizes proportional to the results of their work. In this way elements of market economy were introduced in industry. But these principles of market economy were not appropriate in the context of health care. You could not offer better medical care as a bonus to those who work harder. Nor could you use bonuses in clinics, as it would be impossible to determine, for example, which doctors are more hard-working and more conscientious than others.

As health professionals were not offered any bonuses and, moreover, did not succeed in improving their hourly wages (though they tried repeatedly), they resorted to cutting down on the time given to their patients. Thus doctors examined their patients perfunctorily and referred them to specialists as a rule in order to avoid having to deal with them themselves. The number of patients sent back and forth between various offices grew enormously, causing unnecessary delays in the administration of services, contributing to the creation of long waiting lists and, paradoxically, increasing the total amount of work in clinics. This self-defeating strategy was never abandoned, however, even if a different one proved more effective. Doctors began to seek parallel employment. They could easily make their office hours overlap in two or three clinics, to which they would come late or from which they would leave early. The personnel was instructed to accept only a limited number of visits per day. Needless to say, waiting times grew even longer than before.

Other medical workers, such as nurses, paramedics or orderlies, were paid even less than doctors, and, unlike the latter, could not seek double employment. To make ends meet they began approaching patients with direct financial requests. If they were sly but persistent, they could make an income that topped a doctor's earnings. If they were obvious, they could be discovered and run the risk of being dismissed. At the same time a clinic which adopted a strict policy with the culprits could find itself being unable to hire new personnel. Under the table payments became part of everyday life in medicine and auxiliary personnel stayed away from sanctimonious institutions. State controlled medicine slipped slowly but inexorably into the grey market.

When all this corruption became public knowledge, the government made some half-hearted efforts to eliminate it. In the 1970s two methods were introduced. Stricter financial controls were used in clinics and a new policy was implemented that allowed for an easy creation of medical cooperatives and private medical offices. From then on it was fairly easy to establish private practice in fields such as ophthalmology and dermatology, although it was still impossible in others, such as surgery, which required more numerous personnel or sophisticated equipment.

Economic liberalism solved some of the problems but created new ones. Some doctors could not start private clinics, either because they did not have the initial capital or because they worked in a field where they had to rely on large teams or had to hospitalise their patients for long periods of time. If state clinics remained their only employment, their incomes could be much lower than the incomes of some of their colleagues. Some chose in these circumstances to admit to their wards only patients who would agree to pay an entrance fee. Others developed a largely fictitious private practice and made admission to their clinic dependent on a simultaneous use of their private offices. Still others found ways of making additional income from hospital budgets by passing the patients altogether. The auditors controlled salaries very meticulously, but paid little attention to general clinic budgets. With superficial controls of maintenance and repair, it was often possible to use, for example, building materials, equipment or hospital vehicles for private purposes. In an extreme case a doctor could feed her entire family in the hospital canteen or use the hospital crew to build her own garage with the building materials intended for the renovation of her ward.

The gap between the value of services offered to patients and the declared operating costs of clinics became increasingly larger. Costs grew rapidly, while the quality of service deteriorated. As a consequence the system as a whole became unresponsive to all budgetary incentives. It could absorb large funds and materials without improving the standards of its services; and although it continued to grow in size for many years, it was unable to meet the health demands of the population. In the 1980s in Poland the number of hospital beds per 1,000 population was larger by one-third than in Western Europe. Hospitals were over-staffed, medical and nursing schools produced large amounts of doctors who found it difficult to get employment and large amounts of nurses who preferred to work outside health care, in the chemical industry, cosmetic companies or simply as secretaries. At the same time patient waiting lists grew longer and longer. The system was costly, wasteful and inefficient.

An interesting form of collusion developed between the government and the medical profession. Both sides were aware of the inefficiency of the system and both were unable to solve the growing problems. More crucially, they could never decide what they really thought of the system. On the one hand, they believed that the system was too large and too mismanaged to be reformed with only superficial changes; on the other they thought it was basically sound and needed nothing more than a periodic overhaul. This allowed little room for change and in practice all reforms were reduced to making new investments and to adopting new technologies. Both the government and the medical profession supported investments for reasons of their own. The government hoped that new, better-equipped clinics would make waiting lists shorter. Doctors needed new equipment for different purposes. They wanted to learn new skills – ideally during a visit abroad – to be able to make demands for higher wages in recognition of these skills. The concurrence of interests between politicians and physicians intensified investments in technology and pushed to the sidelines all issues of the proper organisation of health care. Politicians invariably scored high points with their constituencies by announcing that new hospitals would be constructed and the waiting lists would shorten. To most who heard them this non sequitur was far from obvious. Doctors, on their part, got pay increases, contracts abroad, and a chance to treat their patients in front of shining panels with flickering lights. Everybody enjoyed the pageant, and for a long time the magical aspect of medicine belied its functional deficiency.

All these problems notwithstanding, patients on the whole seemed to be satisfied with whatever medical help they could get, whether in state clinics, medical cooperatives or private offices. A survey made in the 1970s showed that approximately 40 per cent of patients used some form of fee-for-service medical care (private and cooperative), while 60 per cent of patients used only state clinics. In the first group 55 per cent were satisfied with the service received (i.e. 'rated it positively'), which compared with 63 per cent of those who found state clinics satisfactory (Ostrowska 1975: 93). The question that one wants to ask in response to these figures is 'Why did so many patients choose what they liked less, and in addition pay for it?' I do not have a convincing answer to this, however it should be said here that the reasons for dissatisfaction may have been different for different people. Some may have been unhappy simply because they were paying, or were paying too much, for the service. Others because they were receiving exactly the same treatment from a private doctor as they would have received in a state clinic. An additional factor could have been that, whereas there is likely to be a state clinic near one's home, it may be necessary to travel farther in order to get to a private clinic.

This last point is interesting in itself. In the 1970s the mean distance in Poland from an average home to the closest clinic was probably the shortest in Europe. Of patients questioned in the same poll 48 per cent said they needed less than fifteen minutes to get to the nearest clinic. This is a very short time, considering that there were few cars at that period. Out-patient clinics could be found in almost every second large village. Only less than 1 per cent needed more than one hour to get to the nearest clinic. Finding a private doctor would probably take more time than that (Ostrowska 1975: 98).

It is most ironic, however, that out of those who so quickly found themselves at the nearest clinic, 56 per cent had to wait for more than one hour inside the clinic before they were received by a doctor (Ostrowska 1975: 98). This shows how inefficient the system was. Apparently it was easier to build thousands of clinics, distribute them geographically, equip them with diagnostic instruments, staff them with doctors, nurses, etc., than it was to enforce predictable office hours for doctors. It is interesting to note here that the number of doctors per 1,000 population in the 1970s was higher in Poland than in most Western countries. Health care management remained for years a completely neglected field.

Inefficient institutions were under constant pressure from disgruntled customers, who unfortunately had no power to initiate changes. They had learned that getting medical care is either a time-consuming or a costly preoccupation. Most were prepared to invest time. They stood in long queues from early morning to register for a visit with a doctor who tried to keep her working hours as short as possible. They flooded corridors of out-patient clinics, and with all this time on their hands, tried to arrange as many visits as possible. Someone with a broken leg would gladly use the opportunity to X-ray her lungs or see a gynaecologist, even on the slightest pretext. It is interesting to note that a similar pattern was observed in Britain immediately after the introduction of the National Health System (NHS): 49 per cent of doctors complained that their patients came only with 'minor ailments', while only 21 per cent said it 'almost never' occurred to them (Gemmill 1960: 51). In Poland, many doctors encountered minor ailments most of the time. This not only exasperated them but also led them to believe that the health condition of the population was better than was commonly thought, which in turn alleviated their scruples about spending too little time with their patients.

All these problems with the nationalised health care system made a debacle inevitable. The system's demise was brought about by insufficient funding at the national level, a lack of effective controls at the hospital level, low discipline among the physicians, a spate of often ungrounded demands from the patients and a sense of *malaise* produced by the numerous but futile attempts to reform a system that was badly managed and extensively developed at the expense of efficiency and quality of service.

DEMORALISATION IN STATE CLINICS

Since 1989, when Poland turned democratic, the future of state-financed medicine has become uncertain. The budget for the nationalised heath care system has dropped a few percentage points annually in three consecutive years. Most clinics have found themselves in a desperate financial situation. Some have closed, some have rented out their space to non-medical institutions, others have simply adopted more heartless methods of warding off their patients. Undercover payments, still considered illegal, have become a routine. Many institutions have found new, ingenious ways of demanding money. For example, a doctor may indirectly ask a patient to pay for X-ray films by blaming the bad quality of the patient's X-ray photographs on the lack of appropriate film. Another doctor may say to her patient that a consultation from a specialist is urgently needed; in the public clinic an appointment can be arranged in a month's time, a private office can offer a consultation immediately. The patient chooses. Most typically, however, the patient pays, or pays extra, simply to be relieved of basic discomforts, for example to have his bed linen changed more often, or to be placed in a more spacious room, to be treated more promptly, or to get a fuller view of his record. As shortage of materials is a fact of life, it is difficult to distinguish between an honest doctor who truly needs some money to complete tests or therapy, and one who simply pockets it.

A survey made in 1994 showed that many patients find 'unofficial' payments acceptable. Of the respondents 77 per cent said that proper care was given only to those patients who paid their doctors directly, hand to hand. Only 18 per cent said that patients would get equal treatment whether they paid or not. (CBOS 1994). These numbers explain why private medicine has become so popular. Fifty-five per cent of the respondents preferred to get their diagnoses and treatment from private doctors. Only 37 per cent recommend state clinics. Two-thirds of those, however, admitted that they made secret payments, while the majority would rather have continued paying in state clinics than go to private ones.

There seem to be two reasons why some of those who are prepared to pay prefer to pay in public clinics, which is illegal, rather than in private clinics, which is the normal procedure. First, fees in private clinics are higher than secret payments exacted for the same service in a state clinic. In private clinics all costs have to be included and taxes must be added. In a state clinic the doctor has already received her salary and the extra earning goes directly into her pocket. She can afford to charge less. Second, a patient who opts for under-the-table payments knows well that the doctor has done something wrong. He may consequently feel free to make bolder demands on the doctor, much bolder than he would dare to make in a private clinic. He may not resort to blackmail, but he may request prompt and efficient treatment, prescriptions for foreign medication, additional tests, or referrals to a reliable specialist of his own choice. Usually all additional favours will be offered at no extra cost.

Overall assessment of the nationalised health care system was exceedingly negative. Only 20 per cent of patients believed that the system was very good, 2 per cent said it was rather good, 33 per cent believed it to be rather bad, and 45 per cent said it was very bad. These are the lowest rates in the entire postwar history of Poland (CBOS 1994). Moreover, the reasons for these negative views are not necessarily connected to secret payments. More and more patients are seriously worried about the professionalism of their doctors. The quality of service deteriorates all the time and professional errors happen too often. Terrifying reports are found in the press. For instance, an ambulance crew carelessly travelled with a patient for a whole night, serving other patients in the meantime, until the man died, because they had mistaken an epileptic attack for the 'strange behaviour of an intoxicated old man'. A clinic in

Warsaw decided to close its AIDS ward and mix the AIDS patients with other contagious diseases, in spite of the protests of doctors who saw this as a dangerous precedent that may contribute to the spread of AIDS in hospitals. Many hospitals fill their beds with patients who have easily curable diseases, because the costs involved are less than if they admitted more serious cases.

The nationalised heath care system has been left with practically no efficient controls. The government has grown tired and disappointed with its own unsuccessful reforms. It avoids issuing stricter regulations or applying stricter controls for fear of bringing the entire system to a halt. Occasionally the Ministry of Health dispatches a circular to all clinics expressing concerns about press attacks on corruption in medicine. Clinic directors summon the doctors and read the circular to them. The doctors vehemently protest and the matter is settled at that.

At the same time, however, the practice of offering high-quality service in public institutions has by no means died out. To this day there are excellent physicians in state clinics who work conscientiously for low salaries. These are model doctors who renounce private joys and devote themselves to their patients. Patients admire them and cite their case as proof that the special calling of medicine is not altogether lost. We may indeed admire the dedication of these doctors. But we should bear in mind that idealists seldom find a great following. J. S. Mill said with reference to the law that it is not made to suit the best but to restrain the worst. The principle can be applied to health care administration. If all doctors were totally dedicated to their patients, if they had no families and no private lives, health care management would hardly be needed. But as most doctors in real life have other ends besides their work, their efforts have to be effectively organised and well paid. A system of health care cannot be based on an idealistic sense of calling.

THE INSUFFICIENCY OF PRIVATE CLINICS

In 1989 a law was passed which provides that anyone may own and run a medical private facility on the condition that the personnel hired to fill medical positions are properly licensed to practice medicine. Health care provision has since then become one more business practice that can bring profit. As I have mentioned, the new clinics are efficient and reliable. They take good care of their patients, make them feel comfortable and safe. They have won themselves a reputation for making proper diagnoses, for choosing effective therapy and for inspiring confidence in their patients. But often they do more. Instead of eliminating a disease, they prefer to 'cultivate it' by turning it into a mild, prolonged condition. That assures them a steady source of income. The practice is hard to detect. Moreover, often it has the full approval of the patient. If this is the case, there is no reason to object. Although ungrounded encroachment on the doctor's time in a state clinic by over-demanding patients is unfair to other patients, in a private clinic no such objections can be raised.

A business-like approach in medicine contributes to an important change in the public perception of disease. Until recently, when state institutions monopolised the field of medical services, the ill or disabled person was seen as being entitled to all necessary professional help. A health problem was not a private event to be attended to using private means, but a sort of natural occurrence, something like a minor flood or earthquake. It deserved the interest of a specialised institution and the sympathy of those who could not help directly. These feelings gave every patient hope and confidence, and enhanced a sense of social solidarity. But the same sentiments encouraged many patients to make excessive demands on the system and contributed to its downfall. Now the pendulum has swung in the opposite direction. The public gives little interest to patients, at least as long as no epidemic seems imminent. Solidarity with those who suffer is gone. Everyone with health problems must struggle on their own.

As the nationalised health care system discharges its functions more and more inefficiently, while private medicine grows increasingly stronger, it seems possible that the mix of services that will be available to Polish patients in the future will be heavily biased towards private medicine. If we keep in mind the central role of medical problems in social life, this change may have a profound cultural impact. Interpersonal relations may be characterised by ruthlessness and cultivated indifference, by a naive belief in the beneficial role of the free market and by the rapacious tendency to profit from the misery of others.

THE 'THIRD PARTY' SYSTEM

The two dominant systems of health care in Poland, nationalised and private medicine, are equally extreme. One is characterised by an unrestricted demand for the best treatment at no cost to the customer, the other requires that medical help is only extended to those who are able to pay. The first is abused by unscrupulous patients who burden it with frivolous demands, and is thus inaccessible to those with serious problems who refrain from displaying them ostentatiously. The second draws a hard line between a person who can easily pay for expensive, supportive or even cosmetic care, and one who cannot even buy essential services. Both systems are equally unethical. It is unethical that a patient who is seriously ill should be denied proper care simply because somebody else abuses the system with silly demands. Similarly, it is unethical that medical help should only be offered to those who can pay for it immediately and in full amount, while those who cannot should be made to suffer interminably. No society should allow that an individual perishes or suffers due to inaccessibility of medical help. It is highly desirable for every society to offer some form of medical assistance to those who need it, as well as to withdraw its support from those who squander its money or abuse its medical institutions.

The Polish system of taxation and health insurance collects enough funds to support a well-designed system of health care for everybody. The employers bring to the Zakład Ubezpieczeń Społecznych [Social Security Administration] (ZUS) an equivalent of 40 to 45 per cent of the total gross salaries paid to the employees. Additionally, every employee pays between 20 and 45 per cent of their earnings as income tax. This means that ZUS and the state budget have at their disposal a fund that amounts to more than one-half of the total purchasing power of the working population. But the payments made to ZUS are used not only to cover medical insurance but also to finance many other kinds of social benefits: retirement pensions, disability claims, unemployment benefits, old people's homes, hospices, etc. The same institutions may also receive financial support directly from the government. This overlapping of financial obligations is rather disturbing.

The total budget of ZUS is annually divided and allotted to specific areas, according to the priorities and regulations of the political party that is in power at the time. This is a relic from the communist system, which pooled all payments indiscriminately in the state treasury and then disbursed the available funds according to the current program of social policy. Banks at that time did not offer loans to investors, as all major investments were made by the government which simply issued new money whenever there was a shortage of state funds. This inflationary procedure eliminated the need for accumulation of capital. Consequently no capital was accumulated and long-term financial commitments were a fiction. Although every employee was made to believe that part of her wages was withheld and kept for her future retirement benefit, no such process had been initiated. No savings were made, and the retirement premiums from the working population were used to pay retirement benefits to those who no longer worked. This practice of direct transfers has not changed to this day. The working population today pays for all current outlays of the state and for all social benefits. To put it differently, there is no functional difference between social security premiums and taxes. Both kinds of payments are used to finance current social policies. The concept of the financial contract between an insured individual and an insuring agency breaks down when applied to the relation between an individual and the state.

Communism has obliterated the difference between social policy motivated by philanthropy and financial obligations which are unconditionally incurred by any agency, state or private, which contracts to take somebody else's money in order to put it to a specific use for some time and return the proceeds to the creditor. Many careless or short-sighted decisions were taken in the past decades because that distinction was blurred. Poland was very tolerant of the squandering of public money, of low accountability and little financial transparency. Exposing these faults now to social criticism might cause much human misery, but leaving the matter as it is only perpetuates old faults. Yet no government after 1989 – whether formed by Solidarity or by the post-communist party – has dared to touch this problem. Retirement premiums are still mixed with social security premiums on the vague promise that they will be paid back from accumulated funds. Still nothing is being accumulated, no such funds exist, and the language used to describe the process is as misleading as it was. No-one is ready to create separate funds for health, retirement, military and police benefits, disability claims and unemployment, etc. We live in the shadow of the all-powerful and all-benevolent state.

Nationalised health stumbles on without benefiting from any major change. It has neither been dismantled and privatised, nor properly financed from a health care fund. Successive governments have locked themselves in indecision, satisfied with vague promises of 'restructuring'. But a real change has not been brought about

139

and will be impossible until a consensus has been reached concerning two issues: 'Who will pay for the new system?', and 'Who will be responsible for its proper functioning?'. It is easy to give evasive answers to them both, and they have often been given in past years: 'Ultimately the insured will pay for health care', and 'The system will be controlled by a 'third party''. In the Polish context these platitudes are not helpful. One wants to have a clear answer to the concrete questions: 'Will ZUS pay for the new system?' and 'Will the Ministry of Health serve as the 'third party''?' Unfortunately many people in Poland would probably be happy if both questions were answered with a 'yes'. They want this because they are tired of inconclusive experiments and want to see the existing institutions work properly. This makes political parties very cautious about any changes in health care.

The fact remains, however, that no social security agency will be able to handle health care insurance properly, as long as it is allowed to transfer funds from one area to another and does not act purely as a health insurance company. A successful restructuring requires that the existing social security administration is divided into several agencies, each founded on its own statute, and each responsible for the administration of only one kind of social benefit. Similarly, the ministry must cease functioning as an agency that does three jobs at the same time: finances some health care services, controls them all and remodels some of them in response to the varying social pressures. No ministry can play the role of a 'third party' if it executes several, incompatible, functions. The 'third party' should be completely released from all obligations other than the purchase of health care services for the entire population. This function may indeed be entrusted to one of the agencies that might result from the dismantling of ZUS, if that ever happens.

VALUES AND VIABILITY

A 'third party' system by definition must be controlled by an agency different from the customers and the providers. The term itself should not indicate, however, that there are three viable options in health care organisation, one favouring customers, another favouring providers and a third favoured by the third party. The customers have no viable option at all. They can control the providers only in very special circumstances: in the army, in clinics that serve some professional groups, such as miners, employees of chemical companies, students, etc. They can demand high-quality services only if they directly employ their doctors. This is impossible on the scale of a whole country. The providers as a group might perhaps muster enough unanimity to control a large scale system, but they have no incentive to do so. They are happy to operate in a free market that has been liberated from all controls, and where the customers have no representation.

So at a national level the only practical option is either to have bureaucratic control by the ministry and its health care specialists, who forecast, plan and provide health services, or to have local agencies that purchase services for the local population from various, competing groups of providers. The first option may be called a 'centralised health care organisation' or a 'nationalised health care system' but not a 'third party' system, even if the ministry claims that it can act as the 'third party'. Any agency that does more or less than it should as a 'third party' should not be considered a 'third party', as it has either too much or too little power to do the job that it is commissioned to accomplish. A 'third party' has only one function to perform: to purchase services for the local population from various, competing groups of providers. A state bureaucracy cannot negotiate the best terms of purchase because it cannot leave aside other governmental considerations. Its inability to perform flexibly and respond quickly to the changing circumstances in real life has been well-documented in literature.

> we cannot rely solely on the profession and its own system of self-regulation to provide a responsible system of care . . . some kind of . . . bureaucratic system is needed . . . since bureaucratic procedures contain their own incipient pathologies, it is important that they . . . allow a great deal of variety and flexibility . . . it is absolutely essential to the provision of humanely satisfying . . . care that the patient be in a position of sufficient independence to be able to exercise choice . . . *individual* rather than organized patients are able to exercise effective influence.
>
> (Freidson 1970)

Systems of health care controlled by central governments cannot be expected to overcome bureaucratic rigidity. They react only to aggregate data, such as rates of incidence of particular diseases, a widespread lack of some sort of equipment, a required level of training in health profession, etc. They cannot differentiate their policies with respect to different regions, age groups, types of patients requiring special care, etc. Thus, simply by virtue of their elevated position, they will either ignore all specific data, or use them by assuming the role of a local and specialised agency, which they then in fact replace.

A 'third party' arrangement works efficiently only in a highly decentralised system of health care, based on premiums paid by all employees, augmented to some extent by premiums from the employers. These funds should be pooled locally to buy services negotiated with the local providers. Purchases should be made by agencies which represent neither the central government nor any of the parties with locally vested interests, i.e. doctors and patients. It is open to debate whether the agency should be a purely professional and independent group of actuarial specialists and physicians, a branch of the local – but not central – government or an insurance company. It is clear, however, that a solution should be adopted that minimises the chances that the 'third party' will develop its own interests. Thus terms of contract should be made public and remain binding for a limited period of time, for example one year. Financial reports should be announced periodically and financial documents should be open to public scrutiny. Obviously these arrangements require a lot of effort expended in negotiating, monitoring, assessing and reporting. A 'third party' system is not 'natural' in the sense that, once created, it will perpetuate itself. On the contrary, it will have to be constantly sustained and supported. If it is not, it will degenerate into a system of lower standards, motivated by partisan interests and operating ineffectively.

If the customers are allowed to exercise excessive influence over it, it may degenerate into a system of inflated health care services, like the one we now have in Poland. The number of services will grow enormously, medical personnel will be too numerous, an average customer will pay too many visits and get too little from them. Second opinions will be sought repeatedly, and the system will pay mostly for cheap and inexpensive medication.

If the medical profession gets the upper hand in the system, it will favour expensive services, impose high fees, take little care of health promotion and preventive medicine. The system will be choked with interesting cases and easily curable diseases – what either arouses doctors' interests or makes low demands on their time. It will have all the characteristic shortcomings of the purely private medicine that does not allow for the introduction of a widespread medical insurance.

In especially grim circumstances the system of health care will relapse into something that resembles folk healing. Alternative medicine will flourish and in extreme cases infanticide may replace contraception and abortion.

In other words, if the functioning of a 'third party' system is distorted, it will turn into nationalised health care, privatised medicine or a substitute for scientific medical practice. It will not continue as a failing 'third party' system. This shows why it is so difficult to create and maintain it. It must win the support of the government, the medical profession and the perspicacious public. It will function well, without relapsing into a different form of organisation of health care, if it does justice to all its underlying values: *social satisfaction, moral commitment to the patient, economic feasibility* and *scientific soundness*. A compromise of any of these values initiates its transformation into one of the cruder versions of health care.

It would be senseless to compare these less satisfactory systems in order to find out which is worse than the others. It may be useful, however, to see why they are all deficient. They all fail because they do not satisfy some of the expectations that are addressed to socially organised health care. These expectations are listed in Table 7.1 below. They have been drawn from the discussion of the basic types of health care organisation presented above. The table is no more than a summary of the positive features that were found in these systems. I make no claim that the features listed are mutually exclusive, equally important or complete. I do not even make the claim – which would be quite remarkable if sustainable – that they are compatible as a whole. I offer them as an intuitive list of prima facie desirable qualities that a viable system of health care has, and in the absence of which a particular system may fail.

I would never opt, however, for piecemeal corrections that might improve one system or another. They are usually impossible, as I tried to show when I discussed the cases of Bomvanaland and nationalised medicine in Poland. My general recommendation with respect to the adoption of a system then is: 1) if there is already a system but it is not a 'third party' system, replace it with one that is and 2) if it is a 'third party system', prevent it from relapsing into anything else. Its problems can probably be cured only by addressing them directly and making the 'third party' as a group of

Table 7.1 Characteristic features of the four types of health care systems

Characteristic features	Type 1: Traditional medicine of Bomvanaland, based on social acceptance	Type 2: Nationalised health care based on the universal right to receive medical services	Type 3: Private medicine based on market principles	Type 4: 'Third party' system combining the values of the other three
1 Are practitioners protected from a flood of minor complaints?	YES, a visit always costs an ox	NO, every visit is free	YES, the fee for service prevents it	YES, through the deductible portion of insurance
2 Is the family engaged in the care of the patient?	YES, the whole family takes a trip	NO, the patient is left alone	NO, the patient is left alone	NO, the patient is left alone
3 Is the practitioner's full potential engaged?	YES, up to the point of exhaustion	NO, doctors can take it easy	YES, it is essential for reputation and further employment	YES, it is essential for reputation and further employment
4 Does the medical profession enjoy prestige?	YES, as magicians	NO, because they are underpaid and inefficient	YES, in proportion to their income and efficiency	YES, in proportion to their efficiency and income
5 Are practitioners rewarded in proportion to their skills and services?	NO, it is always an ox	NO, it is always the same monthly salary	YES, according to the quality of their work	YES, according to the quality of their work
6 Do their incomes fall if they offer ineffectual services?	YES, an ox is sent only when the patient gets better	NO, even substandard service is fully compensated	YES, practitioners must keep their standards	YES, practitioners must keep their standards
7 Do services create pro-health attitudes?	NO, nobody cares	YES, and it makes the system enormously expensive	NO, it is not part of the individual contract	YES, it can be a part of a group contract

8 Are the obligations of the physician conscientiously discharged?	YES, healing is a dignifying event and occurs in full public view	NO, doctors can be sloppy	NO, doctors can 'cultivate' patients and their diseases	YES, competition induces strict professional control
9 Does new technology replace obsolete methods?	NO, tradition does not change	YES, if innovation helps the doctor	YES, if innovation brings higher profit	YES, if innovation is more efficient
10 Is treatment accessible to all who need it?	NO, not every family can offer an ox	YES, if the patient can wait	NO, for some patients, services are too expensive	YES, if a broad system of coverage is used
11 Is the provision of services driven by the patients' needs?	YES, healers do not advertise	NO, the amount of services is controlled by the provider	NO, profits are essential	YES, the amount and quality of services is controlled by the 'third party'
12 Can patients choose their doctor?	NO, there is locally only one healer	NO, the patient must use her local clinic	YES, there are several clinics to choose from	YES, it can be a condition in the contract
13 Can consumer organisations affect the prices of services?	NO, there are no consumer organisations	NO, state institutions do not respond to consumer pressure	NO, private clinics do not respond to consumer pressure	YES, the 'third party' agency balances the demands of the providers and the consumers
14 Can health care managers control the system?	NO, there are no health care managers	NO, there are no health care managers	NO, health care managers only try to maximise profits	YES, health care managers have the means to reduce providers' profits and customers' wanton demands while, at the same time, allowing the system to grow
Number of affirmatives	7	3	7	12

negotiators perform its role fully. Moreover, as there seems to be no alternative superior to the 'third party' system, my recommendation is to try to balance the legitimate expectations of all parties involved, redesign the system when it fails to operate efficiently, constantly monitor and correct its functioning, and ensure that it satisfies its underlying values of social satisfaction, moral commitment to the patient, economic feasibility and scientific soundness.

NOTE

1 Professor Mark Field uses the term 'third party' in a way that I find misleading. For him the three parties covered by the term are 1) customers (patients), 2) providers (doctors and other medical staff) and 3) a state agency, usually a ministry of health, which represents the interests of the customers, and at the same time hires and supervises providers of services. Third party medicine in this sense was at the basis of the nationalised health care systems in Eastern and Central Europe. However, state agencies proved to be motivated by a host of other considerations, for example political, ideological and financial, and, as I argue in this chapter, did not represent the interests of the customers adequately. Consequently, in my own text, I use the term 'third party' to refer to an independent, non-governmental organisation commissioned by customers in order to purchase health care services from providers, and dedicated to solving all problems of health care administration at that level.

BIBLIOGRAPHY

Anderson, O. W. (1972) 'Health services systems in the United States and other countries: critical comparisons', in E. G. Jaco (ed.) *Patients, Physicians and Illness*.

CBOS [The Centre for Opinion Polls] (1994) in *Życie Warszawy* 23 August.

Field, M. G. (1972) *The Doctor-Patient Relationship in the Perspective of 'Fee-for-Service' and 'Third-Party' Medicine*, in E. G. Jaco (ed.) *Patients, Physicians and Illness*.

Freidson, E. (1970) *Professional Dominance: The Social Structure of Medical Care*, New York: Atherton Press.

Gemmill, P. F. (1960) *Britain's Search for Health*, Pennsylvania: University of Pennsylvania Press.

Jaco, E. G. (ed.) (1972) *Patients, Physicians and Illness*, New York: Free Press.

Jansen, G. (1973) *The Doctor–Patient Relationship in an African Tribal Society*, Assen: Van Gorcum.

Ostrowska, Antonina (1975) *Problemy zdrowia i opieki zdrowotnej w oczach społeczeństwa polskiego* [Problems of health and health care in the Polish public opinion], Wroclaw: Ossolineum.

8

ETHICS AND THE MANAGEMENT OF HEALTH CARE IN GREECE

A health economist's perspective

Lycurgos Liaropoulos

INTRODUCTION

Medical ethics has always been important in health system development at different times and in different places. It has long been accepted that morality in health care presupposes equity. It is only recently, however, that in the context of health care the 'immorality of inefficiency' was recognised. Thus, the litmus test of success for health systems and a convenient vantage point from which to discuss ethics from the health economist's point of view is the question of how well a system deals with equity and efficiency.

It has been said, mostly by members of the medical profession, that medicine and economics are difficult bedfellows, mainly because of the different ethical bases on which the two disciplines are founded. Medicine has traditionally been about doing good for the person in need at all cost. Economics, on the other hand, deals with scarcity of resources and their optimal distribution so as to maximise benefit to society. Perhaps the point for a rapprochement between the two disciplines is in the management of health. Management is the function of deciding how, when, how much, and for whom to produce a commodity or service. In the case of health, the management, as political leadership or hospital administration, must make decisions which utilise medical knowledge to maximise the precious commodity of health under the realisation that resources are finite, and that they must be used equitably and efficiently. Because of the involvement of considerations of equity and efficiency such managerial decisions are also ethical.

In this chapter I will examine health reform in Greece during the early 1980s from the viewpoint of equity and efficiency. I will first deal briefly with the issues of equity and efficiency as they relate to health, and then I will give a short overview of the Greek health care system and its evolution. This will serve as background for an ethical examination of the managerial decisions and policies implicit or explicit in the 1983 health reform. My main conclusion is that over-centralisation of decision-making, the politicisation of essentially managerial functions, and a failure on the part of the medical profession to play its proper role lead to inequitable results, even when the main political objectives are overtly egalitarian. The lack of managerial effectiveness also leads to inefficient operation, which further increases inequity in the system.

MANAGEMENT, ETHICS, EQUITY AND EFFICIENCY

I will define as 'macro-management' the functions of planning, directing and controlling the system by the top political and administrative hierarchy, where health policy is designed and most of the important choices are made. This is the natural 'locus' of decisions where ethical considerations should play their most important role. 'Micro-management', on the other hand, is the implementation of policy and the administration of specific programmes and institutions within the health care sector. Here decisions on resource allocation which involve ethical considerations are made, but the field of application of ethics is narrower, since the major policy decisions have already been determined by politicians and top administrators. My main interest in this chapter lies with macro-management. This is because an assessment of health reform from the ethical point of view should concentrate on those aspects of management which most directly influence the design and implementation of this reform.

Equity and, more specifically, the equitable distribution of health care benefits (services) and burdens (paying for these services) are goals in all health systems. However, there is no general agreement as to equity's exact meaning. Some have even suggested that 'equity, like beauty, is in the mind of the beholder' (McGuire *et al.* 1991: 143). But most would agree that equity involves the equal treatment of equals ('horizontal equity') and the unequal treatment of unequals ('vertical equity'). This principle of equality of course lacks substance, as it does not specify what the relevant characteristics are for equal or unequal treatment. Nevertheless, certain substantive properties, such as need or desert, are normally invoked when questions of equality arise, and which of these properties is invoked or given more importance often depends on the particular context. It should also be said here that unequal distribution of health care is not always inequitable, as certain inequalities in health care distribution may be for the benefit of those who are disadvantaged – who possess disadvantageous properties for which they are not responsible (Beauchamp and Childress 1994: 342). Equity in the health system can be discussed at the financing level (the financial burden of services) and at the delivery level (consumption of services).

Equity at the financing level is about 'who pays and how much relative to their incomes'. In an examination of the financial burden for the population or for various socio-economic classes, the yardstick is the degree of 'progressivity' in the financing methods used. A method of financing is said to be progressive when, as income increases, a higher proportion of that income is used to finance health needs. As a major study conducted in ten European countries has suggested, there are four possible methods of financing, listed in decreasing order of progressivity: taxes, social security contributions, private insurance and out-of-pocket payments (Van Doorslaer and Wagstaff 1993). Taxes are considered a more progressive source of financing, assuming a progressive tax system, followed by social security contributions and private insurance payments under certain conditions. Out-of-pocket payments are, naturally, the most regressive form of health care financing.

Equity at the delivery and consumption level is usually about 'what one gets relative to one's needs'. This obviously raises the difficult issue of equal need and of the measurement of need. Besides age groups, there are other population groups with special health problems, for example pregnant women, the mentally ill, or people admitted to a hospital. The question then is 'do these people in fact need more, and, if they do, have we done more for them?'. Equity in consumption of services is often seen as equity of access. Here we look at the geographical distribution of resources such as beds, doctors and other health personnel, facilities and technology, and the cost of procuring their services. Consumption is also seen as expenditure, but this is problematic, since expenditure is the product of price times the quantity of resource use. If a certain population group consumes low-priced services because of heavy state subsidies (as is the case with farmers in Greece), total expenditure may appear artificially low. Finally, equity in consumption relates to the recent debate for a minimum basic care package (Dunning 1992). In most cases, the minimum package is the responsibility of the public sector, with added benefits to be provided on a private basis. This is the application of a minimum equity criterion.

Unlike equity, efficiency is a relatively late comer in the discussion of ethics in health care. The concept of 'efficiency' has often been confused with 'economy', or the tendency to 'economise'. While economy deals with the costs of providing a service, efficiency deals with the relationship between input (cost) and output and/or outcome (benefit). Efficiency seeks to assess what resources are used in providing services and what the services actually produce. It is, therefore, a concept which describes the ratio of total benefits to total costs. It is probably this misunderstanding that accounts for the reluctance of the medical profession and of medical ethics to consider matters of efficiency in the delivery of medical care. The situation has, fortunately, changed over the last two decades. As Jonsen and Hellegers say, 'Traditionally medical ethics has dwelt mostly within . . . the theories of virtue and of duty . . . the nature of contemporary medicine demands that they be complemented by the third essential theory – the common good' (1987: 5). Clearly, the common good is not served if resources are wastefully used. The British Medical Association's *Handbook of Medical Ethics* is even more explicit: 'As the resources available within the NHS are limited, the doctor has a general duty to advise on their equitable allocation and efficient utilisation' (1984: 67).

Two concepts of efficiency figure in the assessment of the performance of health systems. Macro-economic efficiency requires that a certain portion of GDP is devoted to meeting the population health needs. What this portion should be is an unresolved question, but it seems that an expenditure of 8 to 8.5 per cent of GDP is acceptable at a European level. Micro-economic efficiency, on the other hand, requires that production of specific services is carried out at the lowest possible cost for any given level of quality of service. The major sector where such issues arise is in hospital care which absorbs nearly 50 per cent of all health funds, but of concern is also the most efficient mix of services, such as, for example, primary health care and tertiary care. There are various ways of improving micro-economic efficiency, such as by making use of global budgets or of various forms of prospective reimbursement (for example, diagnosis related groups: DRGs) and by introducing market elements into the health system.

Alan Williams makes perhaps the strongest and clearest ethical case for efficiency in health when he writes:

> I even believe that being efficient is a moral obligation, not just a managerial convenience, for not to be efficient means imposing avoidable death and unnecessary suffering on people who might have benefited from the resources which are being used wastefully.
>
> (Williams 1990: 185)

HEALTH IN THE EARLY 1980S AND THE 1983 HEALTH REFORM

It was just over twenty years ago when health became a major political issue in Greece. As rapid economic growth slowed down after the fall of the dictatorial regime in 1974, interest in matters of social policy, hitherto a poor relative to other sectors, became more pronounced. Pensions, traditionally a sacred cow in Greece, consumed a major part of the increase in public social expenditures (OECD 1995). The health sector, on the other hand, under-financed and without a coherent health policy, showed a deficit in the quantity and quality of services offered to many segments of the population. Health was highly privatised, with private payments exceeding public expenditures, and with almost 500 small private hospitals mostly owned by doctors also working part-time in public hospitals. A working party set up in 1976 in the context of national social and economic planning gave a description of the major problems:

- Lack of coordination in the financing and delivery of health services among social security funds hindering the enactment of any health policy.
- Large geographical inequalities in the distribution of resources and services.
- A great deficit in the services offered to the rural population.

- Lack of a policy for infrastructure development in the hospital sector.
- Lack of coordination between the Ministry of Health and other government departments and activities affecting the health of the population.

The working party also found that provider reimbursement systems encouraged inefficiency and promoted induced demand, and for the first time the issue of 'under-the-table' payments was recognised. Three alternative proposals were put forward: 1) the establishment of a national health service 2) the unification of the major social security funds, or their cooperation and 3) coordination in the financing and delivery of services (Centre for Planning and Economic Research 1976).

A consequence of the 1976 Health Report was the health bill of 1980 proposed by S. Doxiadis, then minister of health, which took into consideration many of the findings of the working party. In addition, it proposed the establishment of full-time exclusive employment for some hospital doctors, a network of rural health centres, the promotion of primary health care and public health measures, and the upgrading of medical speciality training (Liaropoulos 1992). This progressive and well-researched bill was proposed by a conservative government at the wake of an upcoming socialist party victory in the 1981 elections. Unfortunately, short-sighted opposition from inside the conservative party on charges of 'covert socialisation', mainly by MPs from the medical profession leery of jeopardising their dominant position, did not allow the bill to reach parliament. Notable is the (historical) fact that the socialist opposition was planning only a token fight in order to 'find the law in place when we become government'.[1]

The socialist party came to power with health reform high on its political agenda, as a response to widespread public demand for change in the delivery of health services. Law 1397, which establishes the national health system, was voted in 1983 as a major reform in the area of health. It coincided with the establishment of national health systems in other Mediterranean countries and with health reforms in many European countries, the basic aims of which were a universal right to health services, a more just geographical distribution of resources and effective cost containment (Abel-Smith 1992).

The main provisions of the law

The 1983 health reform adopted the principles of universal coverage and equity in the distribution of services. The guiding moral principle was the 'de-commercialisation of health', implying greater equity, state responsibility for the financing and delivery of services, and a reduction in the role of the private sector. Cost containment or efficiency was not a main concern, because the magnitude of health expenditures was not known. Instead, the major objective was an increase in public expenditure to 4.5 to 5 per cent of GDP in order to limit the private sector and private expenditure. Efficiency, however, was an indirect goal, implied in the need for the reorganisation of services and improved management. Article 1 of Law 1397 states the guiding principles and basic aims of the reform.

- State responsibility for health services provision.
- Equitable distribution of health services.
- Adequate coverage of the health needs of all citizens, irrespective of age, sex, or ability to pay.
- Decentralisation of services and community participation in decision-making.
- The development of primary health care through a network of health centres and the institution of the family doctor.
- Improvement in the quality of health services and better organisation of delivery from the social security funds.

Health reform was to be implemented through various policy measures, the most important of which were:

- Full-time exclusive employment for hospital doctors and large wage increases.
- Construction of 400 health centres affiliated with local hospitals and responsible for primary health care. Of these 180 were to serve the rural population.
- Establishment of regional health councils with their own budgets and management of health services.
- Significant investment in health infrastructure with the construction of eighteen new hospitals, the upgrading of another twenty, and the upgrading of equipment of all local and regional hospitals.

In some respects, the 1983 health reform was 'outdated', because it did not use experience from other European countries. According to one definition, (successful) health reform implies 'sustained, purposeful, and fundamental changes to improve the efficiency, equity, and effectiveness of the health sector' (Berman 1995: 15). The basic element of reform is expressed by the word 'changes', but the adjectives that precede this further define the process. 'Sustained' means that we provide the means for the implementation of health reform over time. 'Purposeful' means that reform action must consider the opportunities imposed by existing health sector conditions. Finally, 'fundamental' implies the radical change of existing institutional and societal constraints. This definition also allows us to establish certain notions as to what health reform as a continuous process should aim at:

- Strengthening public management.
- Explicit priority setting for a universal package of assured interventions.
- Decentralisation.
- New methods of generating and managing finances for health.
- Enhancing the role of private providers in national health systems (Berman 1995).

As we will see, many of these notions were ignored in the implementation of the health reform in Greece.

THE HEALTH CARE SYSTEM TODAY

System structure

The Greek health care system has always had the main elements of the social insurance (Bismarck) model. Thirty-nine social security funds offer full health insurance coverage by contracting with public and private providers, while the state runs the public hospitals and is responsible for emergency care and the provision of primary care to the rural population. The private sector plays a strong role in hospital, diagnostic and out-patient services.

The legislation of a national health system strengthened the statutory role of government, but a national health service has not been established yet. As a result, the Greek health care system remains fragmented and uncoordinated. Out-patient care is offered mainly through the Social Security Administration (IKA) polyclinics, by hospital out-patient departments and by 10,000 physicians on solo practices reimbursed on a fee-for-service basis by private out-of-pocket payments. Access to basic care is easy, but the process is inefficient with no referral system to other specialities and hospital care. The IKA polyclinics are used mostly by low-income workers for the prescription of drugs or the validation of disability claims. The 180 rural health centres have not reached a satisfactory level of staffing and functional integration with the local hospitals. Finally, solo practitioners are cut off from the rest of the system. Admission to a hospital usually requires referral to the out-patient department, new diagnostic tests, and no follow-up possibility for the primary care physician.

Public hospitals account for 70 per cent of the beds and 80 per cent of admissions. Hospital beds are poorly distributed, and queuing problems exist in Athens, where 30 to 40 per cent of the patients from other areas seek specialised hospital care. Beds are allocated poorly among the various specialities inside the hospital, often based on the director's personal or political 'pull', rather than on real needs. There are serious shortages in intensive care units and other specialised clinical facilities. Despite its relatively small volume of activity, the private sector, and especially a few large hospitals in Athens, is highly profitable due to high utilisation and turnover, and the existence of a strong private health insurance sector.

System administration and management

The 1983 reform did not affect the way the system is managed. Under the Greek constitution, the government must ensure adequate and high-quality services to the population. This has often been interpreted as government responsibility for the actual delivery of care, a position which reached the point of a virtual ban on the private sector in the 1983 health reform. The system is centrally controlled by the Ministry of Health and Welfare, which is responsible for the organisation and provision of health services. Policy-making, financing, and control of even minor staffing decisions are made centrally, and the fifty-two prefectures have little control over resources and local health services. Health insurance is administered through a complex system of public insurance funds in which more than 98 per cent of the total population are compulsorily insured. Each fund has its own administrative, financial and control structure, but government control is decisive, as almost all funds are headed by political appointees. The main form of regulation is prospective control of eligibility and retrospective control of the appropriateness of expenditures as regards coverage. Eligibility and coverage are determined by a legislative mosaic which makes decisions on even the most prosaic matters difficult and time-consuming.

Major problems today

After more than ten years of health reform, health care in Greece today still suffers from lack of credibility and low consumer satisfaction (Ferrera 1993). An excellent synopsis of the major problems is found in the report by foreign experts commissioned by the government in 1994 (Ministry of Health and Social Welfare 1994).

- Weaknesses in public health personnel, programmes and policy measures.
- Unethical practices. The main problems are cost-shifting from the public sector to private payments, especially for hospital (surgical) care and out-patient specialist care, under-the-table payments to doctors to promote prescription of specific drugs, etc.
- Public dissatisfaction and evidence of distrust. This is illustrated by private payments to doctors on the assumption that only in this way can adequate treatment be secured, the bypassing of most ambulance services offered by social security (IKA), and the resulting 'doctor-shopping' for speciality treatment.
- Large geographical inequalities in resource distribution and in the quantity and quality of services.
- Over-centralisation and bureaucratic management at all levels.
- Lack of incentives in the public services, associated with tenure, rigid pay scales and the inability of management to reward (or discipline) staff according to performance.
- Lack of medical records and of an efficient health information system. This makes policy and programme assessment virtually impossible.
- Lack of cost-effectiveness, with open-ended financing, inefficient use of hospital beds, excessive use of drugs and diagnostic tests, and high administrative costs due to the multiple sources of financing.
- Unbalanced mix of staff, with an abundance of doctors and shortage of nurses and other trained staff.

- Lack of quality assurance, appropriateness, and technology assessment.

It is this situation as it stands now after more than ten years of health reform that I will now proceed to analyse from the point of view of equity and efficiency.

THE ASSESSMENT OF THE 1983 HEALTH REFORM

There are certain major variables which determine the functioning of any health system. These are equity in finance and delivery of services and macro- and micro-economic efficiency. By observing changes in these variables over the last ten years or so, we can reach some conclusions on the effectiveness of the health reform, and assess the actual results from the point of view of equity and efficiency in the system.

Matters of equity

Equity in finance

According to data published by the Organisation for Economic Cooperation and Development (OECD), public social protection expenditures in Greece rose significantly from 10.9 per cent of GDP in 1980 to 17.3 per cent in 1993 (Schieber *et al.* 1992). At the same time, as Table 8.1 below shows, there was an increase in total health expenditures between 1980 and 1991, a result of a considerable increase in public expenditure. Private health expenditure increase was modest, but at over 3 per cent of GDP, it was the largest in Europe.

The increase in total health expenditures during the 1980s in Greece was a move in the opposite direction from other EU countries (OECD 1990), where cost-containment policies were put into effect (Abel-Smith and Mossialos 1994), and it was an attempt to compensate for under-financing in previous decades. Public spending increase came almost entirely out of tax-funded government expenditure, changing the composition of public financing between 1980 and 1991 to 60 per cent from tax revenues and 40 per cent from social security. This reflects large government subsidies for hospital care designed to keep down daily charges, in order to

Table 8.1 Health expenditure composition in Greece by source of finance (% of GDP, 1980–91)

	1980	1988	1991
Total expenditure	6.62	7.27	7.86
Public expenditure	3.86	4.51	4.80
of which: 1 tax-funded	1.96	2.63	2.78
2 social security	1.90	1.87	2.03
Private expenditure	2.76	2.77	3.06

Source: National accounts, own calculations

alleviate pressures on social security and discourage the private hospital sector.

This change in public financing has serious equity implications in so far as the distribution of the burden is concerned. Tax-funded government expenditures, paid for by the entire population, cover expenses for farmers and civil servants, who contribute very little towards health insurance funding, while the rest of the population are burdened by heavy social security contributions. As a result, persons who contribute less than their income would justify, enjoy benefits disproportionate to their contribution. Even for the portion of the population which finances its medical needs through social security contributions, however, the existence of considerable government subsidies and the subsidisation of nearly 80 per cent of hospital costs by the state budget introduce elements of considerable inequity.

The degree of inequity in health financing out of taxes is positively related to the degree of regressivity in the tax system. The tax system in Greece is the most regressive in the EU since it depends to a large degree on indirect taxes. To the extent, therefore, that the 1983 health reform was tax-financed, it reduced equity. Moreover, the fact that overall tax revenue in Greece is the lowest in the EU limited the ability of government to finance the public health system and further increased private expenditure. The end result on equity in financing was seriously negative.

Equity in delivery and consumption

The egalitarian jargon of the health reform promised that all citizens would have equal opportunity to use, or have access to, health resources. However, equity at the delivery level is still low among various socio-economic groups and geographical areas. This is due more to resource inequalities on a geographical basis, and less to variations in eligibility and coverage provisions among social security funds. This is shown by the allocation of financial resources, with public expenditures per capita ranging from 18,310 dr. in Central Greece to 43,124 dr. in Athens. It also applies to the allocation of physical and human resources. The staffing of existing health centres varies, with one doctor for 1,510 persons in Attica and one for 3,284 persons in the Peloponnese. Hospital beds vary from 2.9 per 1,000 persons in Western Greece to 6.9 per 1,000 in Attica. Finally, if publicly employed and private doctors are taken together, there are 20,390 in Attica and only 476 in the whole of West Macedonia (Abel-Smith 1994: 87).

Table 8.2 shows that there was a reduction in the concentration of hospital beds, admissions and doctors in the Athens area between 1983 and 1993. This small improvement in the distribution of hospital resources and doctors is probably due to the construction of three university hospitals in major regional centres. Perhaps the major achievement of the health reform was the construction of 180 rural health centres which, despite serious problems of operation and staffing, have improved the availability of out-patient and disease prevention services, thus contributing towards an increase in the equity of distribution of services. The 200 health centres in the urban and semi-urban areas planned in the 1983 health reform were never constructed, however. This creates inequity in the delivery of out-patient care, as the IKA infrastructure is suffering from the problems we mentioned earlier. There are also inequities among age groups. Although Greece has one of the highest percentage of population over the age of 65 in Europe, geriatrics is not a recognised speciality, and there are almost no public long-term care beds. As a result, long-term care of dubious quality is offered on a private basis, and access to it depends on the elderly person's financial position.

Efficiency

Macro-economic efficiency

In order for the increase in public financing to be macro-economically efficient we must not only have an increase in (primary) health resources, but also an increase in the quantity, quality and effective-

Table 8.2 Geographical distribution and use of health resources: percentage concentration in the Athens area (1983–93)

	1983		1993	
	Public	*Private*	*Public*	*Private*
Hospitals	27.9	27.3	29.8	33.9
Beds	50.5	46.9	44.8	53.4
Admissions	45.6	48.9	38.4	57.9
Doctors	61.1	51.7	53.7	49.0

ness of the health services they produce (intermediate inputs). It is only then that we can expect an improvement in the final outcome, which is an improvement in the health of the population. There is a general agreement that the actual employment of primary inputs, or 'bean-counting' as Uwe Reinhardt has very aptly called it, has very little meaning if we want to understand the real forces that shape health system performance (Reinhardt 1993). A good example is the abundance of physicians. Greece, with the highest number of doctors per 1,000 population in Europe, faces problems with over-supply of services and under-the-table deals with other health care providers, while the effect on iatrogenic diseases has not yet been determined. Health resources, however, at least indicate where the health money goes.

In the availability of health resources, shown in Table 8.3, Greece presents a mixed picture. Prohibition of investment in new private hospitals and administered low daily charges during the early 1980s resulted in more than 40 per cent fewer private hospitals, whose resources were not replaced by public beds. Greece, which has 5.1 acute and chronic beds per 1,000 population, faces a shortage of tertiary care public hospitals with special care units such as ICUs, as well as a shortage of amenities and accommodations, or hotel services. This has led to queuing problems, under-the-table payments, and a shift towards large private 'luxury' hospitals, at considerably higher fees.

Human resources, on the other hand, increased substantially, with nursing personnel leading the way, while physician employment also increased by almost a third. It is interesting to note that physicians in private practice increased by more than half, an indi-cation of the growing importance of the private sector in the health economy. The 'glut' of physicians, however, is of little use, given bad geographical distribution, over-specialisation, and a lack of general practitioners. A surplus of doctors leads to over-consumption of drugs and diagnostic services and to practice variations with adverse health effects. The continuing shortage of nurses, on the other hand, is an impediment to system efficiency, because it affects the quality of hospital care and of community and home-based services – all of which are very effective in improving population health status, the effectiveness of preventive programmes and the delivery of health care. With the infusion of new health technologies, the shortage in paramedical and allied health personnel becomes increasingly problematic. In total, and despite the abundance of physicians, Greece employs only 3 per cent of its labour force in the health sector, compared to 5 to 6 per cent in EU countries.

In order to assess progress towards greater macro-economic efficiency I will now look at the final outcome of the increase in inputs

Table 8.3 Primary inputs per 1,000 population and per cent change 1983–93

	1983	1993	per 1,000 pop. 1983	per 1,000 pop. 1993	% change
Total health personnel	75172	112196	7.7	10.9	49.2
Medical doctors	27607	40116	2.8	3.9	45.3
Doctors in hospital practice	13617	18492	1.4	1.8	35.8
Doctors in private practice	13990	21624	1.4	2.1	54.5
Nursing (hospital)	21907	37211	2.2	3.6	69.8
Other personnel (hospital)	25658	34864	2.6	3.4	35.8
Total hospitals	534	368			−31.0
Public	143	144			0.7
Private	391	224			−42.7
Total hospital beds	56759	52414	5.8	5.1	−7.6
Public	35133	37050	3.6	3.6	5.4
Private	21626	15094	2.2	1.5	-30.2
Medical equipment (total units, 1989–93)	2598	4061			56.3
Public	2111	2965			40.5
Private	487	1096			125.0
New diagnostic centres	21	180			757.0
Drugs/capita (IKA)	7.7	7.4			−2.8
Drugs/prescription (IKA)	2.0	2.0			0

Source: National Statistical Service, own data

162

and expenditures. By the health indices used most often, health in Greece is satisfactory when compared with other European countries, and it has improved considerably over the last ten years or so. Table 8.4 shows that Greek people live longer and that mortality from some of the major scourges of our times is lower. Infant and perinatal mortality are still higher than EU figures, but they are among the lowest in the world, and they have fallen very rapidly in the last twenty years.

Do these indices imply an effective health care system, or are there other factors which contribute to this rather rosy picture? To answer, one must look at indices directly connected with health system performance. One such index is avoidable mortality, or the number of deaths from certain causes in certain age groups which could, under normal circumstances, be avoided if the health system in its entirety performed effectively. By these indicators, Greece fared worse than the EU average in only four of the seventeen causes of premature death for the period 1985–9, while, on average, premature mortality was at 58.7 per cent of the EU rates (Holland 1988). However, two causes (hypertensive and cerebrovascular disease [ages 35–64] and ischaemic heart disease [ages 35–64]), which are related to the lack of satisfactory preventive and emer-

Table 8.4 Health indicators and selected mortality indices by cause of death (deaths per 100,000 inhabitants): Greece, EU (1990)

	Greece		EU (12)
	1981	1990	1990
Life expectancy at birth: Men	72.2	74.6	73.1
Women	76.6	79.8	73.9
Infant mortality rate (per 1,000)	17.9	9.7	7.8
Perinatal mortality rate	20.0	12.8	9.4
Maternal mortality rate	5.4	2.6	6.3
Selected mortality indices			
Diseases of the circulatory system	392	367	315
All cancers	171	157	202
Cancer of the lung and of the respiratory system	37	39	41
All accidents	43	40	48
Automobile accidents	15	21	14
Diabetes	31	12	15
Suicides	3.3	3.2	11.3

Source: Holland 1988

gency referral services, are responsible for 46 per cent of the deaths. Taking all this evidence into account, one might conclude that the case for macro-economic efficiency is inconclusive.

It has been suggested that for an assessment of system efficiency greater emphasis should be put into micro-level data (Schieber and Poullier 1991), such as the availability of health technology and its distribution. Biomedical technology in Greece exists in sufficient quantity and quality, but it is unequally distributed and inefficiently used. In the period 1986 to 1991 there were 159 new diagnostic centres, mostly in the major cities, compared with only twenty-one in the previous six years. These were set up in existing private hospitals, or as new businesses, as a response to the ban on private hospital construction after 1983, which led to a search for other investment opportunities. This shift reflected the rapid growth of health technology, especially in imaging, taking place internationally at the same time as the world market for medical equipment grew from $3.2 billion in 1975 to $9.7 billion in 1985 (Thierry 1985). Greece was slow to introduce the new technology in the public sector, but the private sector more than compensated (see Table 8.3, above).

Microeconomic efficiency

The efficient use of resources has always been a major problem. The hospital sector operates on open-ended financing, with no prospective budgeting or cost-based prospective reimbursement. Macro-analysis of hospital statistics in Table 8.5 shows a considerable improvement in utilisation with the public sector leading the way. Overall productivity as expressed by the throughput index (patients per bed per year) improved by over 40 per cent, and there was a significant drop in the turnover interval (the number of days a bed remains empty), from 5.3 to 4.1 days. Improved efficiency in the public hospital sector, however, was mostly due to the elimination of small private hospitals, while utilisation, shown by the occupancy rates, remained low. This is also reflected in differences of efficiency between public and private hospitals. Recent research results show that surgical cases in private hospitals have an average length of stay 40 per cent lower than similar cases in public hospitals (Liaropoulos 1996).

On the other hand, the productivity of out-patient services offered by IKA has deteriorated. Doctor visits dropped by more than a quarter, and drug consumption remained stable, while it

Table 8.5 Intermediate inputs in the production of health services

	1983	1993	% change
Hospital admissions	1186892	1441196	21.4
Public	809551	1165203	43.9
Private	363114	275993	−23.9
Patient days	14367675	13344552	−7.1
Average length of stay	12.1	9.2	−23.9
Occupancy rate	69.4	69.7	0.4
Throughput (total)	21.0	27.5	30.9
Public	23.0	31.5	36.9
Private	16.8	18.0	7.1
Turnover (public and private)	5.3	4.1	−22.6
Doctor visits (IKA)	5.7	4.3	−24.4

Source: National Statistical Service, own calculations

increased for the country as a whole. Since IKA is the main public provider of out-patient services, this means that the population turned to private physicians, a fact with negative equity implications. Most IKA doctors are contracted on a part-time basis on a very low salary scale. Not surprisingly, most of them under-work, effectively recruiting patients for their private practices. Also, they are open to enticements by drug companies or private diagnostic centres in order to supplement their incomes, further reducing efficiency in the delivery of care.

THE MAJOR PITFALLS OF THE 1983 HEALTH REFORM

The lack of 'management mentality' and of managerial ethics

If we refer to the definitions of macro-management and of health reform given above, we can see that health reform in Greece failed to introduce policy elements that would guarantee sustained, purposeful and fundamental change. The responsibility for this failure lies with the politicians and top-level administrators, who shaped the process of decision-making and priority-setting during the period of the 1980s guided by political expediency rather than by criteria of equity and efficiency.

Ineffective management is the main obstacle to efficiency. The 1983 health reform ignored management development and maintained the patronage system intact in an effort to keep all power to the political apparatus. This meant strict control over appointments of staff and procurements, and a refusal to set up planning and evaluation mechanisms concerning financing and service delivery. Manpower planning, technology assessment and quality assurance are non-existent activities, and the whole system is run on political criteria. Hospitals are still run by untrained career civil servants, and members of the boards of directors, each headed by a doctor, are political appointees with no interest in efficient operation. Given the powerful financial incentives for physicians to minimise the time spent in salaried work in favour of private practice, management lacks the power and the incentive to enforce conscientious performance. This results in serious problems of access for patients in public hospitals and out-patient clinics. Moreover, the lack of emphasis on efficient management of the system does not allow questions of equity and efficiency in delivery and finance even to be considered as relevant.

It could reasonably be said that public mismanagement, coupled with the tendency for rigid government control of the health sector, resulted in the development of an ethic of 'indifference' towards the use of resources and their equitable distribution in meeting the population's health needs. The outcome was inefficiency, problems of access and inequity in the administration of the health sector.

The institution of full-time employment for hospital doctors

Full-time exclusive employment for doctors working in public hospitals was the linchpin of the 1983 health reform. The law provided that all hospital doctors were to quit private practice and accept full-time employment with a generous salary raise of 112 per cent. The measure was applied to all grades of hospital doctors in all public hospitals throughout Greece. The ethical basis of the provision was certainly sound. Limited time employment allowed doctors to hold appointments in public hospitals and also to be affiliated with, or even own, a private hospital and run a private practice. This posed serious ethical problems, since doctors used their public position and prestige to practise 'cream skimming' by referring the most 'profitable' cases to the private hospital of their choice. Moreover, their limited involvement in the public hospital often compromised the quality of care and the development of

166

other important activities, such as education, speciality training and research. With public hospitals almost entirely subsidised by tax revenue, this meant large transfers of public resources into private hands.

This rather rigid provision had different implications for doctors, depending on their career stage and professional prospects. Young doctors facing problems of over-supply demanded secure and well-paid employment, while established physicians had fewer incentives to stay within the system. The law, therefore, had three negative effects. First, it forced many of the better-known hospital doctors out of the public system, providing the basis for a highly profitable decade for the private sector. Second, doctors who stayed in the public system eventually developed (illegal) private practices. Third, the state budget was burdened with full-time doctors and salaries not justified in small hospital departments with low patient loads. The end result of this short-sighted and dogmatic policy was to raise the cost of hospital care, to promote inefficient operation, and to strengthen the private sector, which the policy aimed to minimise.

The emergence of a private health insurance market

Since 1986, there has been an upsurge in private life insurance, with annual rates of growth ranging between 30 and 40 per cent. Our research results indicate that the moving force behind this rapid growth was health insurance for hospital coverage (Liaropoulos 1993), indicating widespread dissatisfaction with the public hospital sector and its lack of modern diagnostic facilities. The interest in private health insurance coincided with the implementation of the national health system in 1985, and was certainly not the purpose of a health policy which emphasised public health financing and delivery.

Greece has always had a strong private sector which approaches 3 per cent of GDP. The purchasing power created by private health insurance caused excess demand and higher prices for existing hospital and other health services. It was also a strong incentive to highly profitable private investment, especially after 1989, when the conservative government removed many of the constraints imposed during the 1981–9 period (Kyriopoulos and Tsalikis 1993). Since private services are not reimbursed by social security, we can conclude that the dogmatic attempt to limit the private sector resulted in increased private expenditure, macro-economic inefficiency, and inequitable distribution of resources, as private insurance supplied a market for the private sector against the intent of the 1983 health reform.

The slow rate of adoption and inefficient utilisation of health technology

It has been established that, while health technology is a major cost driving factor (Evans 1983, Waldman 1972), its appropriate utilisation also improves the quality and effectiveness of care. Due to bureaucratic and inept administration, Greece was late to introduce expensive health technology in public hospitals and to make this available in terms of public reimbursement coverage (CABG – coronary artery by-pass graft – was reimbursed as late as 1993). Instead, there was a proliferation of expensive technology financed by private payments (see Table 8.4, for the rate of increase in private and public equipment). In a major EU report published in 1988 six major technologies were studied with regard to the rate of diffusion (CEC 1988). The data are shown in Table 8.6, together with 1993 Greek data from our own research. The table shows that ten years ago Greece was far behind other European countries in the diffusion of technology. After 1986 progress was rapid and, by 1993, Greece had reached or surpassed 1986 European levels. The proliferation of diagnostic 'big-ticket' technology facilities during the last decade, however, has greatly increased public and private health expenditure due to unnecessary utilisation.

The increase of pharmaceutical expenditures and price controls

The 1983 health reform did not include a policy on pharmaceutical care. Responsibility remained with the Ministry of Commerce, and the only policy was price controls – a price freeze on older drugs. As pharmaceutical companies substituted new products for older ones at high prices, social security expenditure during 1981–92 rose by 949 per cent, while the drug price index rose by only 175 per cent. Expenditure on pharmaceuticals increased five-fold between 1987 and 1995, and at 2 per cent of GNP in 1991 it was considerably higher than in other EU countries. This is a classic case of distorted administrative controls leading to results opposite to the intended

Table 8.6 Diffusion of major health technologies in Greece and the EU, (units and procedures per million population) 1982–93

	1982	*1986*	*1993*	*EU(1986)*
Computed tomography (CT)	1.2	1.8	3.8	4
Magnetic resonance imaging (MRI)	NA	0.1	0.6	0.4
Linear accelerators	NA	0.3	1.2	1.3
Renal dialysis machines	155 (1981)	142 (1984)	235	261 (1984)
Lithotripters	NA	0.1	3.1	0.13
CABG	185 (1990)	380 (1993)	615 (1995)	419 (1993)
PTCA	65 (1990)	155 (1993)	278 (1995)	468 (1993)

Source: CEC (1988), own data

ones, as they 'managed' to keep prices low and sent spending sky-high. The end result was inefficiency in the composition of health expenditures and inequity in the system, since 25 per cent of the prescription cost is a co-payment by pensioners and other low-income insured.

CONCLUSIONS AND PROSPECTS FOR THE FUTURE

If the intentions of the 'architects' of the health reform were noble, an effort was also made to 'settle scores' with the medical 'establishment' rather than to introduce change effectively. The young doctors' political power and their desire to play a role hitherto denied them resulted in dogmatic hospital-centred policies which had little to do with efficiency and equity. The medical establishment, on the other hand, did not play a role in shaping the rules of the game, content, as it were, to reap the benefits of a burgeoning private sector, in a vacuum created by public bureaucratic ineptitude and political ineffectiveness. If all of this sounds like a recipe for disaster, that is the story presented in this chapter.

If we want to assess health reform in Greece according to the basic objectives which were identified earlier, we must conclude that very little, if any, progress was made: Public management was not strengthened, as we have already mentioned. Explicit priority setting was practised only with respect to health care for the rural population, but not for the system as a whole, mainly because of the lack of health service research which might have helped in identifying the priorities. Decentralisation is still at the point where it was in 1981, and new methods of financing have not been proposed, except, perhaps, for the relative increase in tax-funded expenditure. Finally, the private sector was not given a complementary role, as in most European countries at the time. In fact, as has been shown, the private sector managed to assume a new and more active role despite the intent of government policy.

Future prospects and some recommendations

The prospects for the future are likely to be more of the same, as it is increasingly obvious that the public sector will remain in the grip of a serious fiscal crunch. At the same time, political impetus for liberalisation is also appearing in the health care market. This will probably take the form of managed care with private health insurance and delivery schemes playing the leading role. There are indications that the private sector is increasing its share of the hospital market, taking advantage of the shortcomings of the public system. This will increase the cost to society and create serious equity problems. If, however, the private sector is allowed to cooperate with the public authorities, it may increase macroeconomic efficiency and equity in the system, as private investment meets the modernisation requirements which public fiscal constraints cannot meet.

Leaving the private sector aside, however, no real improvement in efficiency and equity can be expected as long as public management remains oblivious to the need for fundamental change. System macro-management must undergo thorough restructuring with the following goals:

- Separation of finance from health care delivery with the creation of a national health service and a funding (purchasing) agency.
- Regionalisation of services administration, and delivery and redistribution of resources.
- Promotion of public health and health promotion policies.
- Health personnel development with emphasis on nursing and management.
- Introduction of planning, evaluation and assessment functions.
- Introduction of prospective reimbursement and global budgets in hospital care.

- Amendment of full-time hospital employment for doctors to allow limited private practice in the hospital.
- Elimination of price controls and introduction of a positive list of drugs to curtail pharmaceutical expenditure.

Measures such as the above could 'complete' the unfinished reform of 1983. The public sector in every European country is the major 'player' in the area of health care. However, the only way for the public sector to play its constitutional role as a guarantor of the efficient and equitable provision of adequate and high-quality health services is for it to achieve a significant increase in productivity and quality of care. Whether this will come to pass in Greece is the 'bet' of the next decade (Liaropoulos 1995).

NOTE

1 Private communication to the author by P. Avgerinos, member of the European Parliament, then responsible for health matters of the socialist party and the first minister of health after the socialists came to power in 1981.

BIBLIOGRAPHY

Abel-Smith, B. (1992) *Cost Containment and New Priorities in Health Care*, London: Avebury.

Abel-Smith, B. and Mossialos, E. (1994) 'Cost containment and health care reform: a study of the European Union', *Health Policy* 28: 89–132.

Beauchamp, T. L. and Childress, J. F. (1994)*Principles of Biomedical Ethics*, Oxford: OUP.

Berman, P. (1995) 'Health sector reform: making health development sustainable', *Health Policy* 32: 13–28.

British Medical Association (1984) *The Handbook of Medical Ethics*, London: BMA.

CEC (1988) 'Expensive medical technologies' in B. Stocking (ed.) *Health Services Research Series*, no.5, Oxford: OUP.

Center for Planning and Economic Research (1976) *Five-year Plan for Social and Economic Development in Greece: Report on Health*, Athens: KEPE.

Dunning, A. J. (Chairman) (1992) *Choices in Health Care, Report of the Government Committee*, Rijswiijk, The Netherlands: Ministry of Welfare, Health and Cultural Affairs.

Evans, R.W. (1983) 'Health care technology and the inevitability of resource allocation and rationing decisions – Part II', *JAMA* 249: 2208–17.

Ferrera, M. (1993) *EC Citizens and Social Protection: Main Results from a Eurobarometer Survey*, Brussels: Commission of the European Communities.

Holland, W. (1988) *Atlas of Avoidable Deaths*, 3rd edition, Brussels: European Union.

Jonsen, A. R. and Hellegers, A. E. (1987) 'Conceptual foundations for an ethics of medical care' in L. R. Tancredi (ed.) *Ethics of Health Care*, Washington DC: National Academy of Sciences.

Kyriopoulos, J. E. and Tsalikis, G. (1993) 'Public and private imperatives of Greek health policies', *Health Policy* 26:105–17.

Liaropoulos, L. (1992) 'Health policy: the Doxiadis health bill', *Iatriki* 61: 367–71.

—— (1993) *Private Health Insurance in Greece*, Athens: Forum.

—— (1995) 'Health services financing in Greece: a role for private health insurance', *Health Policy* 34: 53–62.

—— (1996) 'Case-mix variations in public and private hospitals in Greece', unpublished research report, Athens: IMOSY.

McGuire, A., Fenn, P. and Mayhew, K. (1991) *Providing Health Care: The Economics of Alternative Systems of Finance and Delivery*, Oxford, OUP.

Ministry of Health and Social Welfare (1994) *Report on the Greek Health Services*, Brian Abel-Smith (chair), Athens: Ministry of Health and Social Welfare.

OECD [Organization for Economic Co-operation and Development] (1990) *Health Care Systems in Transition: The Search for Efficiency*, Paris: OECD.

—— (1995) Social Data File, Paris: OECD.

Reinhardt, U. E. (1993) 'Competition in health care, or deconstructing the debate on health policy', paper presented at the EHMA Annual Conference, Warsaw, 29 June – 3 July.

Schieber, G. J. and Poullier, J. P. (1991) 'International health spending: issues and trends', *Health Affairs* 10, 3: 22–38.

Schieber, G. J., Poullier, J.P. and Greenwald, L. M. (1992) 'U.S. health expenditure performance: an international comparison and data update', *Health Care Financing Review*, 13, 4: 1–88.

Thierry, J. P. (1985) 'Technology and the future of health systems', paper presented at the international meeting on 'Future of Health and Health Systems in the Industrialized Societies', Bellagio, Italy.

Van Doorslaer, E. and Wagstaff, A. (1993) 'Equity in the finance of health care: methods and findings' in E. Van Doorslaer, A. Wagstaff and F. Rutten (eds), *Equity in the Finance and Delivery of Health Care: An International Perspective*, CEC, HSR Research Series no. 8, Oxford: Oxford Medical Publications.

Waldman, S. (1972) 'Effect of changing technology on hospital costs', *Social Security Bulletin* 35: 28–30.

Williams, A. (1990) 'Ethics, clinical freedom and the doctors' role' in A. J. Culyer (ed.) *et al. Competition in Health Care: Reforming the NHS*, Basingstoke: Macmillan.

9

REGULATION OF THE FRENCH HEALTH CARE SYSTEM

Economic and ethical aspects

Jean-Claude Sailly and Thérèse Lebrune

INTRODUCTION

In this chapter we discuss, from the point of view of health economics, the ethical implications of the attempt to control health expenditure in the context of the French health care system. In the first section, following a short overview of the essential characteristics of the French health care system, we focus on the increasing growth of health expenditure and describe the problems resulting from its control. In the second section, in view of the difficulties caused by this control, as well as the arguments that are so often given to show that it is unethical, we try to demonstrate that the regulation of health expenditure is by no means unethical and that it is possible to reconcile ethics with a consideration of the economic aspects of health provision. This enables us, in the third section, to study the nature of the reforms to be implemented in the future, with a view to reconciling their economic aspects with ethics. In this section we also give an exposition of, and morally evaluate, the reforms which are currently being implemented.

THE FRENCH HEALTH CARE SYSTEM: ITS CHARACTERISTICS, THE GROWTH OF EXPENDITURE, THE PROBLEMS OF CONTROL

The foundations of the present French health insurance system were laid down in the Acts of October 1945, which covered wage-earners in commerce and industry and called for the adoption of a system of universal cover. It took thirty years to implement this system: it was extended to farmers in 1961, to the self-employed in 1970 and to the whole population in 1978. Today it is estimated that only a very small percentage of the population (less than 400,000 people) is not covered by health insurance.

The main characteristics of the French health care system

Major principles

The system is based on three major principles:

- Universality, which involves the transfer of goods and services from the healthy to the sick and from the working population to the non active members of the society. It also involves payment of contributions on the basis of earned income and not according to the risk of illness.
- Liberalism: the existence of a large private sector characterised by the freedom to practice, the freedom of patients to choose their practitioner and the freedom to prescribe.
- Pluralism with regard to finance, the supply of health care, and the modalities of control.

Health insurance schemes

Three main schemes cover 95 per cent of the population:

- The General Scheme (the National Health Insurance Fund/Caisse Nationale de l'Assurance Maladie – CNAMTS), covering 80 per cent of the population, namely the majority of employees in the private and public sectors. This system is jointly managed by the employers and the unions.

175

- The Agricultural Mutual Fund (Mutualité Sociale Agricole – MSA), covering 9 per cent of the population, essentially farmers and agricultural wage earners.
- The Health Insurance Scheme for Self-Employed Persons (Assurance Maladie des Professions Indépendantes – AMPI), covering 6 per cent of the population, notably the self-employed.

Eight other insurance systems cover the remaining 5 per cent of the population. These health insurance systems are almost entirely funded by social contributions.

The organisation of health care services

Primary care services are provided by private practitioners: 114,000 physicians as of 1 January 1996 (61,000 general practitioners and 53,000 specialists); 30,000 dental surgeons; 26,000 dispensing chemists. Physicians can practice in two sectors: either in sector 1 (83 per cent of general practitioners; 66 per cent of medical specialists), in which medical fees and rates of reimbursement to patients are fixed; or in sector 2, in which physicians determine their own fees and patients are reimbursed on the basis of the reimbursement scale of sector 1.

Hospital care services are provided by two kinds of hospital: public hospitals (1,052 establishments, 344,000 beds) and private hospitals (2,312 establishments, 189,000 beds) in which 56 per cent of the beds are managed on a profit-making basis. Private hospitals often specialise in specific treatments, such as, for example, surgery and obstetrics.

Rules for reimbursement

In general, except where reimbursement involves third-party payment, patients pay the provider of health care directly and are reimbursed afterwards by the Social Security Department (provided that the patient is so entitled, which is the case for 83 per cent of those insured), on the basis of a prescription charge which varies according to the type of care dispensed. Thus, in 1995 Social Security covered 89.6 per cent of hospital and medical unit expenditure, 57.1 per cent of primary care provision and 57.9 per cent of medical goods.

The funding of health care services

Funding is provided as follows (1995): 73.6 per cent by Social Security (whose resources come essentially from social contributions which amount to 20 per cent of earnings for the General Scheme, of which two-thirds are borne by the employers and one-third by employees), 0.8 per cent by the state, 6.6 per cent by complementary insurance and 19 per cent by households.

Private practitioners receive a flat-rate remuneration. Private hospitals are paid on the basis of tariffs which are negotiated every year. Hospital doctors receive a flat-rate remuneration. Public hospitals and private establishments which cooperate with the public authorities have been financed since 1985 by a global annual allowance linked to a rate of growth fixed by the Ministry of Health.

The rapid growth of health expenditure in France and problems of control

In 1995 national health expenditure in France amounted to 782 billion francs. Compared with GDP this total (9.9 per cent) put France in second place among the countries of the OECD (after the United States of America), but in first place among the countries of the European Union (EU), ahead of Austria and Germany (9.6 per cent), The Netherlands (8.8 per cent), and well ahead of Italy (7.7 per cent) and the United Kingdom (6.9 per cent).

This high level of health expenditure corresponds to one of the fastest growth rates in the OECD. Already during the period 1976 to 1990 it was clear that France was different from other countries, in that it maintained one of the highest growth rates (5.3 per cent per annum in volume), exceeding by 79 per cent the growth rate of its GDP. This situation became more pronounced during the 1990s. After the cuts which took place from 1986 to 1988 (under the Séguin Scheme), growth recovered and the increase in health expenditure exceeded the growth of GDP by a factor of 2 in 1990 (elasticity equal to two[1]) and by a factor of 3 between 1991 and 1993. The situation in France differs from that in countries such as Germany, Denmark or Luxembourg where elasticity of expenditure is close to 1; or even countries such as Japan, Ireland, and Sweden, where elasticity was smaller than 1 over the same period. Nevertheless, since 1990, there has been a deceleration in expenditure (+6 per cent in volume for total medical consumption in 1991, +4 per cent between 1991 and 1993, +1.8 per cent in 1995). However, since these years correspond to a period of reduced growth of the GDP, or even recession – as was the case in 1993 – this reduction in the growth rate did not lead to a fall, but rather to an increase in the elasticity of health expenditure compared to GDP (equal to 3 in 1991; to 2 in1994).

Why is it so difficult to control health expenditure?

Among the reasons why it is difficult to maintain this expenditure are, doubtless, certain organisational characteristics of the French health care system,[2] even though some of these characteristics have undergone changes recently – in particular since the beginning of the 1980s and the implementation of the clinical (vs budgetary) control of health expenditure, and since the reforms of April 1996.

The system is governed by two authorities – the Ministry of Health and the Ministry of Social Security – whose areas of responsibility are hospital care and primary care respectively. In addition, the system seeks to reconcile 'free market' principles and state intervention. Because of this duality of authority and principle, the various elements of the health care system lack consistency and, moreover, opposition is generated between two types of activity. The first is restricted, in a rather irrational way, by a ceiling on expenditure, while the second is relatively free from any such constraint. It follows that the elements of economic control which are introduced into the system are either of limited efficacy or are themselves limited.

As far as hospital regulation is concerned, the global financing allowance established in 1983 makes it possible to control hospital expenditure, at least in establishments belonging to the public sector or cooperating with the state. (Thus there has been a reduction in hospital care as a proportion of total medical consumption from 53 per cent in 1983 to 48.4 per cent in 1995.) But this does not mean that resources, thus distributed, are optimised: historically the fixing of funding arrangements has contributed to a perpetuation of discrepancies between hospitals, which are not always justified by the activities of these establishments. We still lack appropriate analytical tools to identify hospital activities and to be able to adjust financing to needs (although the introduction of the Medical Information System Programme/Programme Médicalisé du Système d'Information – PMSI effects methods of financing hospitals from 1997 onwards). We also lack adequate mechanisms to ensure the involvement of medical practitioners in the definition of hospital strategies as well as in the determination and management of the means allocated to various hospital units.

In primary medicine, the combination of a demographic increase in the number of patients, flat-rate remuneration for treatment and extremely flexible conditions for the distribution of medical technology is leading to a considerable increase in expenditure. The absence of health care access systems enables patients to have direct access to specialists, thus contributing to a marked increase in the activities of this type of practitioner. Indeed, the number of specialists increased by 66 per cent between 1980 and 1995 as against 38 per cent for general practitioners. Also the number of technical treatments (e.g. radiology or laboratory tests) is increasing considerably in some specialisms (e.g. gastroenterology or cardiology).

Ineffective measures

Since 1975 various attempts have been made to control the growth of health expenditure, in particular through the adoption of various schemes:

- Attempts to control some aspects of health care supply: for example, the creation of a health map in 1970 indicating the number and distribution of hospital beds and heavy equipment or the introduction of a quota system for admissions to medical schools in 1970. Although these policies were along the correct lines, they did not succeed in controlling the supply of health care services, either in the hospital or in the primary care sector.
- Measures to reduce prices: constraints on daily hospital charges until 1983; recalculation of the key items on the treatment list (consultations, visits, specialised treatments); fixing the cost of drugs; establishment of guidelines for increases in the global funding allowance granted to hospitals – the global budget being in itself a measure enabling the control of both prices and the quantity of treatments; adoption of rules for the evaluation of flat rates for admissions to private hospitals; flat rates for drugs; flat rates for operating theatres. Following the creation of Sector 2, measures were implemented from 1980 onwards enabling

doctors to avoid price constraints without increasing the share of expenses borne by the community.
• Measures specifically targeted at consumers in order to increase their financial liability: increase in prescription charges (the portion of the cost of medical treatment borne by the insured); scrapping reimbursement for certain drugs; establishment of a hospital flat rate for admissions.

Figure 9.1 clearly indicates the perpetuation of the discrepancy (even if this is due, in recent years, to the weakness of economic growth) between the growth rate of expenditure and the growth rate of the GDP, and highlights the difficulty of controlling health expenditure in France. In the past, after each recovery plan, it was possible to observe a temporary slackening of the growth of expenditure, followed shortly after by a further increase in the rate of growth.

Conclusion: is it not desirable to introduce reforms in order to ensure a better control of expenditure?

The inadequate control of the French health care system has had certain undesirable consequences. First, due to the constant increase in expenditure, public authorities are trying to limit the increase in reimbursements made by social security bodies. This policy is of course increasing the share borne by patients.[3] Second, the financial difficulties encountered by public institutions are leading to the adoption of rationing measures, the effect of which is a reduction in the quality of medical care.

In general, we think that the French health care system, which used to be ranked among the first in industrialised countries, is in the process of losing ground in terms of global cost-efficiency, universality and quality.

It is important to put an end to the progressive running down and fragmentation of the system. This requires better control and a further rationalisation of health expenditure. However, the question is whether this process is ethical.

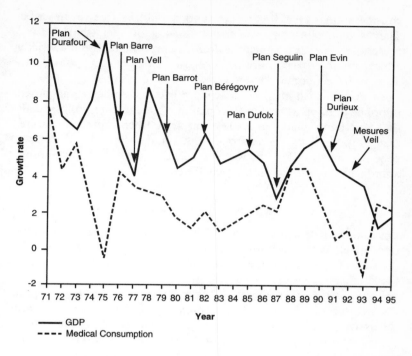

Figure 9.1   The evolution of the annual rate of increase of real GDP and
real total medical consumption in France (in French francs)
with indications of the various plans for changes to the health
insurance system in France
Source: OECD-CREDES (1996)
Note: Bottom line represents GDP. Top line represents medical consumption

IS IT UNETHICAL TO CONTROL HEALTH EXPENDITURE?

Health care providers are extremely cautious, indeed anxious, about
the increasing importance given to economic considerations in decision-making processes, both collective and individual. They are
inclined to think that the desire of government, managers and
economists to introduce a greater degree of economic control into
the health care system runs counter to medical ethics: how can we
risk introducing financial criteria in a domain as vital as health? Is
it not offensive to deny health care services in the name of economic

considerations? Health care providers should be free to prescribe. They should consider only the well-being of their patients and prescribe whatever treatment is deemed appropriate. From a strictly ethical point of view, care providers are not obliged to take into account the economic consequences of their decisions.

In France, such ideas are so widespread and so deeply anchored in public opinion as well in the opinion of health care professionals that no attempt has been made to bring out their erroneous nature. Our purpose is to demonstrate that, on the contrary, there is a coherent relationship between medical, ethical and economic approaches, and that it is desirable to reconcile them.

Ethics and economics

Let us note that there are similarities between the oft-quoted definitions of ethics and economic science: the art of making choices in the case of the former; the science of making choices in the case of the latter.

Ethics is the art of making choices based on values (e.g. respect for life, freedom, human dignity, solidarity, truth). These values are themselves hierarchically organised and derive from principles (e.g. the categorical imperatives of Kant, of which the best-known statement is 'Do not do as you would not wish to be done by').

Economics is the science of making choices, of optimisation. The two disciplines are rather similar in their approach, in that both seek to identify the best means to reach specific objectives within certain constraints. Where they differ is in the manner of obtaining knowledge (economics adopting the scientific method) and in the nature of the aims and objectives that they pursue (economics being exclusively concerned with the production and distribution of wealth).

For the economist specialising in health issues, the basic problem to be solved may be summarised as follows: how can we ensure the highest possible level of health within a given budget? In what economic system for the organisation of production? With what methods of pricing and funding? With what system of distribution of funding?

In view of this, the objectives and concerns of health economists are closely related to those of health care providers, who also seek to create a maximum level of health among their patients while taking due account of the constraints imposed upon them – for example, the state of technology, the time available, the prioritisation of emergencies, etc. Far from being opposed in their objectives, then, the medical and economic approaches are complementary.

As to the alleged moral conflict between medical decision-making and economic constraints, it can be argued that, on the contrary, these two different considerations can be morally reconciled.

If resources are scarce, they must be efficiently used. If health is considered to be a precious asset, strenuous efforts must be made to use the resources allocated to it in the best possible way. Undoubtedly economic parameters must be introduced into the medical decision-making process. With limited resources we cannot do whatever we want, at any time and for any patient. This, if carried to the extreme, would in fact be counter-ethical. Choices must be made – resources granted to one patient cannot be simultaneously given to another. The ethical approach demands that the available budget for health care is distributed, between the various categories of patients, as well as between therapies, in a way which ensures the maximum level of health.

This kind of preoccupation was already shared by health care providers at a time when there was no social security system. The creation of the latter, which was of course necessary, desirable and beneficial, led in effect to a weakened awareness of economic considerations.

The socialisation of the system and the weakening of economic considerations

In view of the importance we attach to health, the uncertainty about when a disease might occur and how serious it might be, and the consequent desire to have access to all types of care, industrialised countries have devised an organisational structure for health care which is based on the idea of social security systems. By introducing a third agent to the interaction between patient and health care, that is, the social security system, which is responsible for insurance against risk and is specially designed to break the direct economic link between patient and care provider, industrial societies have sought to attenuate and conceal the economic aspects of health care, both for the patient ('Will I be able to pay for such and such a treatment?') and for the care provider ('Will my patient be able to pay for the treatment that I may prescribe?'). This disguising of the economic aspects of health care, which reflects an obviously commendable concern for social cohesion, is a credit to our societies, which have in this way managed to develop a high-quality health care system available to all.

However, if we carry the concealment of the economic aspects of health care too far, the system runs the risk of becoming less efficient – of generating a smaller volume of health than could be achieved with the resources allocated. This, it seems, is what happened in France throughout the two periods outlined chronologically below, the first being a time of 'sedative' misconceptions, the second being a period of misunderstanding, conflict and opposition. In what follows, after a brief look at these two periods, we will outline a third period, towards which it would be desirable to move, and in which new kinds of relations could be established, after a process of cross-fertilisation which we regard as necessary.

The rise of the health care system

The first period, which corresponds to the rise of the French health care system, covers the three 'glorious' decades, 1945 to 1975, characterised by a convergence of interests of all those involved in the system (government, health professionals, social security bodies and patients covered by national insurance). Due to continuous economic growth and the progressive extension of social cover, the social security system was able to finance all expenses claimed for reimbursement. Public authorities had a stake in the creation of employment, the modernisation of hospitals and the improvement of the health of the people. There was a considerable increase in the number, power, and income of health professionals. Patients and those insured took better care of their health, while they were well covered by social provision.

This period was marked by a significant increase in the number of private cars, television sets, household appliances, teachers, houses, motorways, doctors, and hospital beds, without being subject to restrictive budgetary constraints. Given that at this time limitations, although present, were not stringent, and conflicts were not acute (since everybody generally obtained what they wanted), choices facing people were less harsh, and therefore to a certain extent less visible.

The emergence of financial problems

This first period (1945 to 1975) ended with the appearance of severe constraints, which became felt towards the end of the 1970s, and which led to the dismantling of the previous consensus. From then on, the interests of the various groups involved in the health care system started to diverge. Public authorities had to face other growing needs (e.g. education) or new challenges (e.g. unemployment). They moreover feared the escalation of social contributions as this would weaken the competitiveness of the country. Health professionals, who were now more numerous, saw their interests become increasingly divergent, particularly in view of their need to keep their clients and protect their incomes (general practitioners vs specialists; primary vs hospital care; public hospitals vs private clinics). The Department of Social Security became obsessed by the budget deficit, as it was now unable to balance its books to meet the high level of expenditure. Patients covered by national insurance attempted to resist any reduction in cover and insisted on having access to increasingly expensive health care services.

In this increasingly fragmented situation fundamental concepts became more and more conflicting: thus we can see an opposition between:

health care (worthy)	vs	costs (unworthy);
health carers (who care)	vs	economists or administrators (who manage);
the right to health	vs	the cost of health;
universality	vs	efficiency;
dedication	vs	responsibility;
the individual	vs	the group;
individual patient	vs	public health care;
ethics	vs	economics.

During this period, economic considerations were rejected in the name of ethics: health care professionals wished to do the maximum, at any time and for all patients, without considering the economic consequences of their actions. The period was characterised by increasing divergencies and by conflicting opinions related *inter alia* to the development of policies geared to the control of health expenditure. Needless to say, this situation in France is only a case of a more general phenomenon found throughout the industrialised world.

The creation of a new perception

We must now go beyond the conflicts of the second period and concern ourselves with how patient care can be reconciled, within an ethical framework, with a concern for economic considerations.

This reconciliation has become a necessity in view of the explosion of needs that our health care system will have to face in the near future; needs linked to the acceleration of technological progress (e.g. the cost of the commercial introduction of new compounds: up to one billion francs, in some cases; equivalent to 1 per cent of all pharmaceutical expenses!) or the emergence of new pathologies (e.g. AIDS or Alzheimer's disease), at the same time that considerations of competitiveness make it impossible to increase the burden of compulsory deductions.[4] In the area of social security, given that the means of funding cannot increase in an unconsidered way, problems such as unemployment or the payment of old age pensions will become increasingly acute in the future, further reducing room for manoeuvre with respect to the funding of public health expenditure.

Taking into account the simultaneous increase of needs and constraints, it is of the utmost importance to ensure a more effective distribution of available resources. Thus, we must distance ourselves from the stages through which we have passed hitherto:

• The stage at which it was possible to provide an increasing number of services without being particularly concerned with their economic implications – a period of relative affluence dominated by the notion of medical progress.
• The stage at which clinical, patient-oriented considerations were placed in opposition to economics – an attitude which has led to disintegration.

Instead we should move towards a period in which we seek to reconcile different approaches and opinions within a framework of rationalisation. The broader perspective we propose does not imply any impoverishment (e.g. of patient care), but will, on the contrary, lead to a process of enrichment.

A rise in the level of the health of the population should be seen not only in connection with what the health care system can offer but also in the light of other, external factors. Thus one's health may be improved by one's culture, education and lifestyle. (In France, according to HCSP (1994), 40,000 deaths per year are due to habits which are avoidable.) The health care system itself is capable of increasing the level of health of the population through the implementation of various initiatives (e.g. preventative medicine) and by being open to new approaches and strategies. Many alternatives may be here envisaged, both outside and inside the system, and our aim should be to select those which generate the greatest benefits on a cost-effective basis.

It is clear that we can benefit from a more multi-disciplinary approach in the implementation of health initiatives and health policy: health care providers, epidemiologists, economists, psychologists, sociologists and managers are called upon to work together in order to enlarge their vision and bring valuable inputs into the project of increasing the level of health of the population. What is for certain is that an ethical approach makes it necessary for health care providers to re-introduce economic parameters into their decisions, to ensure that their practice becomes more effective both in the quantity and quality of health services rendered.

WHAT TYPES OF REFORM WILL MAKE IT POSSIBLE TO RECONCILE EXPENDITURE AND ETHICS?

In this third section, we shall consider the reforms which have been in the process of being implemented in France since April 1996. We shall study their characteristics and highlight the ethical issues which they raise: see HCSP (1996).

Curbing the rate of health expenditure

From the point of view of ethics, there are two reasons why this policy is essential. The first relates to what actually contributes to the improvement of health. Apart from the health care system – which, according to estimates, has in France contributed only to a 10 to 20 per cent reduction in mortality since 1960: see HCSP (1994) – three additional factors play an even more important role. These are the degree of social cohesion of the population, lifestyles and working and living conditions. When we think of how to prioritise the use of funds available, it then becomes essential that we place more emphasis on those courses of action which aim to strengthen, for example, people's potential in the professional and educational fields, than on injecting additional funding into the health care system.

The second reason derives, in the French case, from the detrimental effects to health that ultimately result from an excessive and ill-controlled increase of health expenditure. In order to cope with an increase of health expenditure which exceeds the rate of growth of GDP, it is necessary either to raise the level of national insurance contributions (which tends to increase labour costs, reduce employment and therefore aggravate social exclusion), or decrease reimbursements (thus putting a brake on the access to health care of the underprivileged groups in our society). In both cases, the effects on the general health of the population can be negative, as social inequalities are aggravated.[5]

It appears then that the economic necessity of controlling health expenditure (a necessity that relates to concerns about employment and economic growth) is also an ethical necessity, as it relates also to considerations that are connected to the state of public health.

Looking at the recent state of affairs in France, the reduction (by 3 points in 15 years) of the total expenditure reimbursed by social security[6] as well as the increase in deductions (almost doubling of the Generalised Social Contribution/Cotisation Sociale Généralisée – in 1993) did not prevent a considerable deficit in health insurance in 1995. This deficit is leading to new measures of the same type. Gradually, a consensus is emerging: health expenses borne by the community should be determined beforehand by the public authorities and not established after the event, as has been the case for most primary health care expenditure.

The rulings of 1996 tend in this direction. As of autumn 1996, parliament must fix the national rate of increase for health insurance expenditure, which will then be divided between the hospital and primary care sectors. Clearly this allows constraints to be placed upon the global supply of health care.

Redefining the role of the state in relation to social security funds

According to Soubie *et al.* (1994), the state has the following responsibilities in the context of health care:

- To define public health objectives (which must be targeted, quantified and made public).

- To set financial targets (see above).
- To ensure the quality of health care.
- To guarantee access to quality care (which involves the definition of rules by which the community assumes responsibility for care).

There has been a clear strengthening of the role of the state since the beginning of the 1990s. This is reflected in the following: the creation of a High Commission for Public Health/Haut Comité de la Santé Publique – HCSP, in 1991; the adoption of measures aimed at curbing the growth of primary care expenses (see below); a first attempt at defining health policy (HCSP 1992; 1994); the extension, in May 1995, of the remit of the Ministry of Health (which is now also responsible for financing the Health Insurance Scheme).[7] Among the projects in progress are the definition of a national health policy (which presupposes a broad approach and the adoption by the country's elected representatives of the strategies decided upon); and the implementation of a regional planning programme by means of Regional Health Organisation Schemes/Schémas Régionaux d'Organisation Sanitaire – SROS.

As to the responsibilities of the health insurance funds, these must be obviously redefined in the light of the changes in economic and social circumstances. While there is a general consensus in favour of entrusting to these funds the management of the health policy defined by the state (the granting of the funding required to meet health objectives, the creation of regulatory mechanisms, guaranteeing equal access to health care), many experts are still wondering whether it is possible to maintain the joint participation (parity) of employers and trade unions, and are even proposing to replace the latter by the insured themselves.

The 1996 reforms redefine these responsibilities. In the context of the reforms it is intended that there should be 'agreements between the state and the Social Security Departments extending over several years covering targets and management policy'. In the area of health, these agreements 'fix the rate of increase of health care expenditure in urban areas, so that it is a function of the national rate of health insurance expenditure increase fixed by Parliament'. These agreements also determine 'the direction taken by government action over several years in the areas of public health, medical demography, and medicines'. All this is designed to ensure a better fit between the supply of health care and the distribution of resources on the one hand, and the government's stated objectives on the other.

The agreements on targets and management policy are implemented at local level by means of contracts extending over several years between the national funding bodies and local funding bodies, except in the case of the agricultural scheme. The regional boards of the health insurance funding bodies (set up by the reforms) define within the areas under their jurisdiction a common policy for the management of risk, while respecting the laws covering social security finances, and the agreements on targets and management. This is particularly the case in the domain of urban health care.

The overall aim of the measures contained in the ruling relating to the organisation of social security is to put in place procedures which will enable the supply of health care and the availability of resources – at both national and local level – to match health needs and the ground rules set out by government more closely.

Revising the mechanisms for regulation

In 1992, Professor C. Beraud, National Medical Adviser to the CNAMTS, published a controversial report on the utility and quality of some categories of health care provided in France (see, on this issue, Beraud 1994; 1995). According to his diagnosis, 20 per cent of the care provided was useless, or even detrimental.[8] The majority of experts and political figures agree that the French health care system must be more closely regulated; and the present trend is for the medical profession to implement control of health expenditure.

Following Beraud (1995), we may define the regulation of a health care system as involving a set of administrative, budgetary, economic and clinical mechanisms, which, on the basis of essential information generated by the system, enables the feedback which is necessary for the continuous improvement of the quality of care and of the general health of the population.

Two conditions must be fulfilled in order to put in place such a regulation:

1 Information must become available on the following: health in general and the factors affecting it; the functioning of health care units; diagnostic procedures and therapies; medical practice; the

impact on health of the system in relation to health care expenditure.

2 On the basis of the above information, the rules of the organisation, charges and finance (including the appropriate sanctions) must be worked out in detail, in order to enable the system to make optimal use of available resources.

In relation to the first of these, the French health care system suffers from considerable deficiencies. While we have administrative information on the functioning of health care providers (the number and types of hospital beds, the duration of hospitalisation, the number and type of treatments performed in primary care), we have very little information on hospital output and medical practices (the types of illnesses treated, the nature and cost of proposed therapies) and, *a fortiori*, on the quality and efficiency of these practices.

Various efforts are currently being made in order to mitigate these failings. Some of them concern the hospital sector. Public hospitals and establishments cooperating with the public sector must from now on submit information on their activities by preparing, for each patient, a document entitled Standardised Discharge Report (Résultat Standardisé de Sortie – RSS). As an experiment, this system has been tried in the region of Languedoc-Roussillon. It is presently being extended nationwide. It is proposed that, after a few years, the financing of hospitals will be based, at least partly, on the findings of this evaluation procedure. This kind of approach may create considerable difficulties with regard to the distribution of funds within current guidelines (under which the rate for the annual increase is applied virtually uniformly to all establishments). Analyses of the findings so far indicate that the distribution of funds between the most favoured hospitals and those which are least favoured may vary on a scale from a budget index of 80 to 120 (for identical activities).

Other initiatives relate to primary care. Since 1994, the Medical Agreement (Convention Médicale) between the health insurance bodies and the doctors' unions defines good medical practice with respect to prescriptions[9] in various circumstances (Références Médicales Opposables – RMO). Failure to observe these definitions results in the financial sanctions stipulated in the agreement. In addition, a decision has been taken in favour of the coding of medical treatments and the creation of medical files. In exchange for their acceptance of the RMO (and thus of a certain degree of control over prescriptions) as well as for their pledge to moderate their expenses, medical unions have obtained an increase in their remuneration (+10 per cent over two years). As to private hospitals, they have been obliged to comply with a national quantified objective (since 1991) and the fees charged by laboratories and nurses have been subject to global package agreements.

How can we evaluate these reforms? If we look at the figures, we notice that, initially, their implementation was quite successful: in 1994, for the first time since the beginning of the economic crisis, the growth rate for total medical consumption (+3.3 per cent) was lower than the growth rate of the GDP (+4.1 per cent).

If we consider all types of expenditure, we see (again in 1994), a relatively small increase in medical practitioners' allowances (+2.7 per cent) and in the prescription of drugs (+1.8 per cent). More importantly, we see a reduction in laboratory testing (−7.2 per cent). The reduction in medical prescriptions in urban practices (drugs and tests) was noted even before the signing of the agreement, at a time when medical practitioners were convinced that it was impossible to control, and therefore to sanction, individual practices. This seems to indicate that there is a tendency to comply whenever regulation concerns excessive prescriptions and is matched by positive economic sanctions (an increase in practitioners' fees). It is generally agreed that the reduction in the growth rate of primary care expenditure did not cause a deterioration in the general health of the population. It appears then that the adoption of the principle of collective moderation of expenditure did not conflict with the interests of patients. However, the figures for 1995 and 1996 indicate a further acceleration in the growth of primary care expenditures.

Among the changes in practice or alterations to the system that must come about, some will affect the consumer, others those responsible for prescriptions, and others still the general organisation of the system. As far as consumers are concerned, it seems necessary to restrict the freedom they have hitherto enjoyed, namely that of consulting their doctor of choice as many times as they wish. This freedom has had a two-fold disadvantage: on the one hand, in some cases it has created excessive demand for consultations and visits; on the other, it has increased competition between care providers, and has therefore prevented them from practising in a more cost-conscious manner. Amongst the measures recommended in this area are: the creation of a patient medical record to be presented upon each visit, a requirement that the patient chooses a family doctor for a specified period (one year, for example), and a ban on direct access to specialists. In the 1996 reforms only the creation of a health record was decided upon.

As to those who are responsible for prescriptions, it is essential, in the first instance, to implement certain arrangements enabling their activities to be monitored. One such arrangement is the Medical Programme Information System (Programme Médicalisé du Système Informatique – PMSI) in the context of hospitals and proper coding of medical treatments and test results in the primary sector. While the development of the Medical Programme Information System is already well under way, the coding of medical treatments in urban areas (which was decided upon in the 1996 reforms) is encountering difficulties which are political and cultural rather than technical.

No rational regulation is possible until we achieve these measures and the information they provide. As long as health professionals do not accept control of their practices, regulation will be difficult and it will be impossible to ensure proper clinical control of expenditure.

In addition to the responsibilities they have towards their patients, prescribers should be made aware of the responsibility they have towards the community as a whole, since it is indirectly through their observance of agreements with the community (social security) that they acquire the right to obtain resources from it.

Finally, we must review the rules pertaining to the allocation of funds. Hospitals should receive their funding on the basis of actual performance. In this context two important measures are proposed under the reforms. First, resources provided for hospital treatment at national level will be shared out on a regional level in such a way as to reduce the significant inter-regional inequalities which may be observed in the current distribution of funding. Second, regional hospital agencies will be created at regional level, whose task will be to negotiate, with every hospital establishment, contracts regarding objectives and resources. The setting up of these agencies should eventually lead to an adjustment of funding as a function of performance, which itself will be redefined in terms of needs.

In the field of primary care, the reforms of 1996 propose setting the rate of expenditure increase in urban areas annually, thus allowing for a possible repayment of a portion of their fees by health professionals in the event of their exceeding the fixed target.

In summing up the situation in France with regard to the control of health expenditure, we should note the following:

- France is one of the developed countries (excluding the USA) which, until recently, placed little emphasis on a policy of expenditure control, except in the hospital sector (since 1985).

- This policy is particularly difficult to implement in France because of the organisational characteristics of its health care system on the one hand (dual responsibility, lack of coherence), and the marked resistance of professionals in the primary sector, whose ideas are underpinned by an extremely liberal concept of the practice of medicine, on the other.

- For these reasons, it is difficult to persuade all concerned to accept the necessity of regulating health expenditure, even if they are shown the ethical nature of such regulation. However, in view of economic necessities and the growing difficulties of financing health expenditure, positions on this issue are changing.

- Regulatory arrangements are being put in place, notably following the reforms of 1996. These are of an essentially cost-cutting (remaining in budget) nature in the hospital sector (although this will change with the work of the regional hospital agencies), and of a more clinical nature in the primary sector.

- In order for the reforms which have been introduced to succeed in reconciling the pursuit of patient care with financial constraints through the setting up of efficient and prudent medical practice, it will no doubt be necessary to effect a Copernican revolution in the minds of health professionals. Indeed, one of the major conditions for successfully developing the health care system resides in persuading the medical profession that, in the interest of patients, they must practice in a prudent and cost-conscious manner.

- The fear remains that in the absence, for the time being, of tools which would allow the regulation of costs by the medical profession itself, and in view of the profession's resistance to change its attitudes and working practices in accordance with what is required by this kind of regulation, we will have to move, for some years to come, in the direction of a form of control of the health care system which is essentially based on cost-cutting. This is the direction towards which we will have to go, even if first experiments in clinical control carried out in the primary sector are encouraging. This could only be to the detriment of ethical considerations.

NOTES

1 The elasticity of health expenditure in relation to GDP indicates the percentage increase in health expenditure for a 1 per cent increase in GDP. When this elasticity is equal to 1, expenditure is increasing at the same rate as GDP. When elasticity is higher than 1, it is increasing more quickly (twice as quickly if elasticity is equal to 2). When elasticity is less than 1, health expenditure is rising more slowly than GDP.

2 See on this question Soubie (1993), HCSP (1994), Moto (1995).

3 Thus, in France between 1980 and 1994, the proportion of national health spending borne by social security went from 76.5 per cent to 73.5 per cent, and that borne by families from 15.6 per cent to 19.1 per cent.

4 Compulsory deductions, i.e. direct taxes and national insurance contributions in France, amount to 44 per cent of GDP. This level is 4 points higher than that observed on average in the EC. It exceeds by 6 points the level for Germany and the United Kingdom, and by 13 points that for the United States and Japan.

5 In the opinion of certain experts, Japan's good performance in terms of health indicators may be due, to a considerable extent, to the low degree of inequality and the high level of social cohesion observable in that country.

6 Although France was in thirteenth position only in the OECD's 1993 list dealing with the proportion of the public financing of health expenditure. This proportion was 74.4 per cent for France, while it was, for example, 82.6 per cent for Denmark, 83 per cent for the United Kingdom, 88.9 per cent for Belgium, and 93.3 per cent for Norway.

7 Ministry of Public Health and Health Insurance.

8 Several examples of this are given in the context of systematic accounting: when twelve tests are performed using automatic equipment, there is only a 54 per cent probability that all the tests will be normal in a person who is in good health. Pre-operative tests carried out upon entry into the hospital are useless in 97 per cent of all cases. The mere fact of having to write down those indications which justify the prescription of clinical tests could reduce their number by 40 per cent, thus creating a saving of five billion francs.

9 The definition of best practice is the responsibility of a college of experts under the supervision of the National Agency for the Development of Medical Evaluation (Agence Nationale pour le Développement de l'Evaluation Médicale – ANDEM), which under the 1996 reform became the National Agency for Accreditation and Evaluation in Health (Agence Nationale d'Accréditation et d'Evaluation en Santé – ANAES).

BIBLIOGRAPHY

Beraud, C. (1994) 'Le développemennt continu de la qualité des soins', *Le Courrier de L'Evaluation en Santé* 4: 2–17.

—— (1995) 'La regulation du système de soins', *Le Courrier de L'Evaluation en Santé* 5: 2–23.

OECD-CREDES (1994) *Eco-Santé 1994*, Paris: CREDES.

HCSP [Haute Comité de la Santé Publique] (1992) *Stratégie pour une politique de Santé*, Edition Ecole Nationale de la Santé Publique.

—— (1994) *La Santé en France*, Paris: La Documentation Française.

—— (1996) *Rapport du HCSP à la Conférence Nationale du Santé*, Paris.

Moto, L. (1995) 'Santé et multidisciplinarité, choix et décisions', *Hermès*: 294.

Soubie, R. (1993) *Santé 2010. Rapport principal et travaux d'atelier*, Paris: La Documentation Française.

Soubie, R., Portos, J. L. and Prieur, C. (1994) *Line Blanc sur le système de soins et d'assurance maladie*, Paris: La Documentation Française.

INDEX